Athenian Popular Religion

JON D. MIKALSON

Athenian Popular
Religion

THE UNIVERSITY OF NORTH CAROLINA PRESS

CHAPEL HILL AND LONDON

Both the initial
research and the publication
of this work were made possible in part
through grants from the National Endowment for
the Humanities, a federal agency whose mission is to
award grants to support education, scholarship, media
programming, libraries, and museums, in order to
bring the results of cultural activities to
a broad, general public.

© 1983 The University of North Carolina Press

Manufactured in the United States of America

93   92   91   90   89   7   6   5   4   3

Library of Congress Cataloging in Publication Data

Mikalson, Jon D., 1943–
Athenian popular religion.

Bibliography: p.
Includes indexes.
  1. Athens (Greece)—Religion.   1. Title.
BL793.A76M54   1983   292'.08   82-25616
ISBN 0-8078-1563-2
ISBN 0-8078-4194-3 (pbk.)

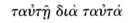

ταύτῇ διὰ ταῦτά

C O N T E N T S

Contents

PREFACE

This book presents what Athenian people, apart from poets and philosophers, said about their gods and religious beliefs in the late fifth and fourth centuries B.C. The gods and religious views of Homer, Pindar, Aeschylus, Sophocles, Euripides, Plato, Aristotle, and other philosophic and literary masters have been widely studied for generations, in some cases for centuries. But such studies are, fundamentally, treatments of Greek theological and intellectual history. Athenian writers clearly expected their audiences to be familiar with current literary treatments and philosophic theories about the gods and religion, but the question has remained open of the extent to which their audiences shared these views and made them a part of their religious life. It was this question that led me to collect, from what I judged to be reliable sources, the religious beliefs and attitudes that were publicly expressed and casually accepted by the great majority of Athenian citizens.

What emerged from this collection was a surprisingly consistent and homogeneous corpus of popular religious beliefs. Amidst remarkable multiplicity and variety of rituals, myths, and cult figures the Athenians maintained rather straightforward, simple, and self-consistent ideas of what the gods provided for them, what was expected of worshippers, what was pious and impious, and so forth. These popular beliefs often lack the intellectual and metaphysical dynamism of the theories of "intellectuals" of the time, but a recognition and understanding of them is of fundamental importance to our view of Athenian society. This understanding will also substantially aid

our efforts to describe and appreciate more fully both the traditional and the innovative elements in the handling of religion
by creative thinkers such as Euripides and Plato.

Two works, Jean Rudhardt's *Notions fondamentales de la pensée religieuse et actes constitutifs du culte dans la Grèce classique* and
Kenneth Dover's *Greek Popular Morality*, have been especially
helpful to me. They provide good collections of material and
also clear much of the ground. I have, in some ways, done less
than they with this same material, but in this instance a less
ambitious approach may produce a more sound and useful
study. Dover and Rudhardt each incorporate numerous poetic
sources into their discussions of popular religion. It is, I con-
tend, better methodology first to determine from reliable evidence what can be proved to be popular belief. Only after this
has been satisfactorily accomplished can we isolate and evaluate
statements of popular beliefs or allusions to them in the poets
and the philosophers.

I intend to provide a descriptive study of Athenian popular
religion and have not introduced current psychological and anthropological theory and speculation concerning Greek religion. It seems that accurate description must precede theoretical
interpretation, and that both prosper when they are somewhat
independent. Sound and independent description permits us,
as we read studies in Greek religion, to recognize more clearly
when we are moving from the descriptive and analytical to the
interpretive, the theoretical, and even the fantastic. It will also
allow us to distinguish better what was common and wide-
spread in religion among the Greeks and Athenians from what
was idiosyncratic and peculiar even to them. Such distinctions
are of the utmost importance, particularly in the complex and
protean subject of Greek religion.

The completion of this work was made possible largely by
the support of the National Endowment for the Humanities
and of the University of Virginia. They provided the means
for a precious year of uninterrupted work. That year was spent
at Cambridge University, where the pleasure of my stay was

greatly enhanced by the kindnesses of Geoffrey Kirk and John Morrison. In particular I wish to thank A. Geoffrey Woodhead who, with his colleagues at Corpus Christi College, provided such warm hospitality. I am also grateful to the readers of the University of North Carolina Press and to the others who have offered valuable suggestions and criticisms.

JON D. MIKALSON
University of Virginia

A B B R E V I A T I O N S

The names and works of classical authors are abbreviated in the text and notes in general accord with the system in the *Oxford Classical Dictionary*[2]. Modern works cited frequently in the notes have been assigned a short title; full citations appear in the Bibliography.

AJP	*American Journal of Philology*
BCH	*Bulletin de correspondance hellénique*
BSA	*Annual, British School at Athens*
CP	*Classical Philology*
CQ	*Classical Quarterly*
CR	*Classical Review*
Erchia, calendar	G. Daux. "La grande Démarchie: un nouveau calendrier sacrificiel d'Attique (Erchia)," *BCH* 87 (1963), 606–610.
FGrHist	Jacoby, Felix. *Die Fragmente der griechischen Historiker*. 3 vols. in 14 parts. Berlin and Leiden, 1923–1958.
GRBS	*Greek, Roman, and Byzantine Studies*
HSCP	*Harvard Studies in Classical Philology*
HTR	*Harvard Theological Review*
IG	*Inscriptiones Graecae*
JHS	*Journal of Hellenic Studies*

MH	*Museum Helveticum*
Nilsson, *GGR* I³	Nilsson, Martin P. *Geschichte der griechischen Religion*, vol. I³. Munich, 1967.
Peek, *GV*	Peek, Werner. *Griechische Vers-Inschriften*, vol. 1. Berlin, 1955.
RE	*Real-Encyclopädie der classischen Altertumswissenschaft*. Edited by A. Pauly, G. Wissowa, and W. Kroll.
RhM	*Rheinisches Museum*
SEG	*Supplementum Epigraphicum Graecum*
TAPA	*Transactions of the American Philological Association*
Tod, *GHI*	Tod, Marcus N. *A Selection of Greek Historical Inscriptions*. 2 vols. Oxford, 1946–1948.
YCS	*Yale Classical Studies*

Athenian Popular Religion

O N E

Introduction

The general character of Greek religion and the nature of the ancient sources that happened to survive have made it surprisingly difficult to determine the religious beliefs and attitudes of the "ordinary" ancient Greek. Our sources for Greek religion tend to fall into two groups: firstly, the poetic and philosophic, and secondly, the scholastic and archaeological. The writings of poets and philosophers have provided the raw material for numerous studies of ancient Greek religious thought, but these studies, based as they are on creative literary works, really treat theology and the development of Greek intellectual thought, not the religion of ordinary people. We learn of many important details of Greek ritual and cult practice from the ancient scholarly tradition as it is preserved in the *Suda* (X A.D.) and other ancient lexica compiled by Harpocration (I–II A.D.), Hesychius (V A.D.), and Photius (IX A.D.). Similar "scholarly" explications of religious terminology and ritual are provided by scholiasts whose notes and explanations survive in the manuscripts of some classical authors. These various scholastic sources, especially when they can be supplemented by epigraphical and other archaeological material, sometimes allow us to give a reasonably complete description of what the ancient Greek *did* in cult practice. But they scarcely ever offer any sure indication of what the individual *thought* or *believed* when he performed these cultic acts.

What we should most welcome, of course, is a "confessional"

literature in which individuals spell out their own religious beliefs and detail those points in which they differ from conventional beliefs. But such a literature is alien to Greek religion. So too is the concept of a book of revelation, such as the Bible, that sets forth what a person should believe. The Greeks also did not have a national or state church or a centrally organized priesthood to put forward and promote religious dogma. We thus lack for the Greeks convenient sources for what the ordinary person was expected to believe.

We must also remember that the ancient Greeks resided in several hundred small city-states that prided themselves on their independence from one another. In varying degrees Sparta, Corinth, Thebes, Athens, and the other city-states differed from one another in political, social, and economic structure, and it is only reasonable to assume that they also differed to some extent in their religion. We know from Pausanias' travel guide of the second century A.D. and from modern studies that myths and cult practices varied considerably from one city-state to another, and one has every reason to assume that religious beliefs also may have differed significantly.[1] One should be wary of assuming that a religious belief or practice must have been current in all the city-states and among all Greeks simply because it is attested for one city-state.

Religious beliefs and attitudes, however conservative they may have been, must also have changed throughout the centuries. Historical sense would suggest, and the evidence indicates, that there was a considerable difference between the religious beliefs of, for example, the Athenian of the sixth century B.C. who saw the beginning of the construction of the temple of Zeus Olympios and the Athenian of the second century A.D. who saw its completion under the Roman emperor Hadrian.[2] The names of the deities and many of the cult practices remained the same throughout these centuries, and this tends to conceal changes in religious belief. But the religious beliefs did change, and in studying Greek religion we must distinguish carefully between those held in different time periods as well as in different city-states.

This book focuses upon the religious beliefs and attitudes attested for Athens during the late fifth and fourth centuries B.C., approximately from the end of the Peloponnesian War (405) to the death of Alexander the Great (323). Athens alone of the city-states can realistically form the subject of a general study of religious beliefs, because from her alone do we have anything more than the most meager scraps of evidence for religious history. The late fifth and fourth centuries are the most promising period for such a study, because in comparison with other periods, fairly abundant evidence for social history exists in surviving political and forensic orations and in the inscriptions. By limiting the study to Athens of the late fifth and fourth centuries I hope to avoid the inaccuracies and contradictions inherent in the synoptic approach to Greek religion, an approach that sometimes indiscriminately amalgamates evidence from widely disparate places and historical periods.

This is not to claim that beliefs and practices discovered in this period were necessarily limited to it. Some originated before it, and some continued to exist far beyond it. Some did both. On occasion in discussing a statement of religious belief or practice I refer to a source from an earlier or later time, but only if the belief has been attested to for the period in question. My intent throughout is to avoid attributing to the late fifth and fourth centuries beliefs and concepts that have their proper place in an earlier or later time.

This book concerns "popular" Athenian religious beliefs and attitudes. "Popular" is not used here to indicate "middle-class" or "lower-class" in social terms,[3] nor is it being used in a pejorative sense. This study does not treat the Greek peasant whose private and communal religious practices and beliefs Martin Nilsson has so carefully and sympathetically described, but investigates rather what Nilsson terms the popular religion of the townspeople.[4] It focuses on religious views and attitudes that were acceptable to the majority of Athenians of the late fifth and fourth centuries. These are the views and beliefs which were a part of the common cultural experience of the Athenians and which were spoken of and acted upon daily by average

Athenian citizens. They form, as Guthrie puts it, "the routine of religion which was accepted by most of the citizens of Athens as a matter of course."[5] During the late fifth and fourth centuries many innovative and idiosyncratic religious beliefs and theories were being developed and discussed by literary and philosophic figures, and these have been studied extensively by scholars. I have excluded these from this study, unless it can be demonstrated that they had an impact on popular religious belief *during this period*. Some philosophical and religious theories, and in particular those of Plato, did influence later times, but unless the influence is detectable during this period, they have been excluded.

Descriptions of individual deities, of cult practices, and of festivals will also be very limited, being used primarily to clarify statements of religious belief. In default of clear and convenient statements of popular beliefs, many scholars of Greek religion have concentrated their efforts on objective descriptions of deities, rituals, cults, and festivals, and have occasionally attempted to extrapolate from these descriptions the feelings and motives of the worshipers. This study differs considerably from such studies in that it directs attention first to what the Athenians said (τὰ λεγόμενα) about their religion and treats what they did (τὰ δρώμενα) only to the extent that it clarifies or illustrates what they said.

I have introduced little of recent sociological, anthropological, and psychological theory about Greek religion. In Greek ritual and myth particularly there are fossilized remnants of much earlier, primitive practices and beliefs. Since the late nineteenth century there have been numerous attempts to build upon these remnants theories about Greek religion, theories which usually derive from current work in the social sciences and which are supported by parallels from other cultures. It is my view that descriptive work should precede theoretical interpretation and that both prosper when they are reasonably independent. It is also wise for us to know clearly what the Greeks consciously said about their religion before we begin to mine the somewhat murky depths of their subconsciousness. My intent is to present a descriptive study of one aspect of Athenian popular religion and to leave it to others to create a comparative, theoretical approach to it. I do not mean to disparage the theoretical work being done in certain areas of Greek religion, because excellent insights and valuable material have been offered by scholars such as E. R. Dodds in *Greeks and the Irrational* and Walter Burkert in *Homo Necans*. But in the study of popular religion the need now is for some descriptive work; a theoretical bias would only impede this work.

The primary ancient evidence for this study is threefold: the orators, the inscriptions, and the historian Xenophon.[6] Although the importance of the orations of Demosthenes, Aeschines, Isocrates, Lycurgus, and others as a source for popular ethical and religious beliefs has been noted from time to time, it was only comparatively recently that they have been given their proper place in the study of these matters.[7]

The orations presented in the law courts and the citizen assemblies are the best evidence available for popular religious beliefs of the period. In the law courts the speakers addressed juries of from five hundred to twenty-five hundred or more Athenian adult male citizens, who were chosen by a rather complicated allotment process. A jury was not, of course, a perfect cross section of the Athenian citizenry, and the elderly, the urban, and those of the lower income groups may well have been somewhat overrepresented. This, at least, is suggested by the caricature of jurors in Aristophanes' *Wasps*.[8] In addition these trials were held only in the city, and the pay for jurors was comparatively meager.[9] But nevertheless, next to the ecclesia, the Athenians' general legislative assembly, the juries of the law courts represent the best cross section of Athenian society available to us.

The speakers in the law courts attempted to plead their cases as persuasively as possible and surely took care not to alienate the jury. The speaker would either naturally or with calculation express moral and religious views which would find acceptance with the greatest number of the jury. The plaintiff or defendant in a lawsuit could hardly be expected, like Plato's Socrates in the *Apology*, to risk losing his case for the sake of making telling political, moral, or religious statements. The numerous surviving forensic orations indicate all too clearly that the single purpose was to win the case, and for this it was necessary to express sentiments intelligible and acceptable to the majority of the jurors. We may, therefore, assume that religious views and beliefs expressed in these forensic orations were familiar and acceptable to the majority of Athenian citizens of the period.

Political orations are generally viewed with somewhat more skepticism than forensic orations as evidence for the beliefs of ordinary citizens.[10] Their exhortatory character, their occasionally idealistic patriotism, and our own experience with speeches of politicians justify this skepticism. But in the expression of religious views they may, I think, be used as reliable sources. An Athenian political orator such as Demosthenes, although he may have been attempting to reform popular opinion about economic policy, war, treaties, and such matters, was not attempting reform of religious views. Rather he used generally accepted religious beliefs as elements of persuasion to support his cause. And since this is the case, the religious views and beliefs expressed in these political orations may be assumed to be familiar and acceptable to the majority of the citizens.

From this period survive numerous writings which have a semioratorical form but were never intended to be presented orally to a group of citizens. They were composed as showpieces by rhetoricians and philosophers[11] and have their origins in the writings of the fifth-century sophist Gorgias. They are usually heavily tinged with contemporary philosophical theory and for this reason must be treated with caution as sources for contemporary popular beliefs. Into this category fall several works of Isocrates, as, for example, his panegyric of Helen (10). In this study these semioratorical writings are used only to detail religious beliefs which are attested from more reliable evidence.

It is my intent to illustrate religious beliefs which were generally familiar and acceptable to the majority of Athenians. In using the orations for this purpose, it should be noted that orators appeal to socially acceptable beliefs. These may, on occasion, be at variance with what the people or a substantial minority of the people did believe. For Athens of the period, of course, we entirely lack "confessional" literature which might reveal significant differences between private beliefs and those which were publicly acceptable.[12] We get rare glimpses of these differences in criticisms of contemporary religious beliefs and practices by intellectuals such as Plato and Theophrastus. On occasion these criticisms contribute to our understanding of popular belief and will be incorporated into the discussions.

Most inscriptions, inscribed on stone and publicly displayed, were directed to the general citizenry. They include cult regulations and prohibitions, calendars of festivals and sacrifices, economic and legal matters concerning cults and sanctuaries, honorific decrees, dedications to deities, and epitaphs. These inscriptions seldom present explicit statements of religious beliefs, but they do occasionally offer excellent contemporary illustrations of their application. For this reason I have included, either in references in the notes or in translation in the text, a representative selection of epigraphical texts from the late fifth and fourth centuries.

The writings of the intellectuals such as Euripides, Plato, and Aristotle are introduced only sparingly, either to illustrate a belief already attested from another source or to present their occasional descriptions of popular beliefs. Without clear evidence from reliable sources the religious theories and views of philosophers such as Plato and Aristotle cannot be assumed to have been widely accepted among the people, unless we choose to disregard the risk of creating a hopelessly romanticized picture of the average Athenian. An even greater caution is required in the use of the dramatists. When we are often unable to determine whether a specific passage or speech illustrates the views of the poet or has been given to the character only for dramatic purposes, we are hardly justified, without external evidence, in assuming that a given passage reflects popular religious views. The tragedies are, moreover, set in mythical times, and to a certain extent the mythical element has conditioned the religious aspect.[13]

The comic poet Aristophanes, however, has been widely used in studies of Athenian social history. Some scholars who quite properly reject the tragedians as sources for popular customs and beliefs because, as Aristotle (*Po.* 1448a16–18) puts it, the tragedians represent man better than he is, nevertheless use Aristophanes extensively as a source.[14] One must be cautious, I think, and take to heart Aristotle's further remark that comic poets represent man worse than he actually is.[15] W. K. C. Guthrie, in fact, used the character Dicaeopolis of Aristophanes' *Acharnians* as the focal point of his description of the popular religion of the period.[16] However much Dicaeopolis may have prided himself on being a "good citizen" (*Ach.* 595), I can only think that the solemn speaker of Lysias' seventh oration and the embattled speakers of the orations composed by Isaeus would have been appalled to be likened to Dicaeopolis. He may be likeable as a comic figure and we may feel some sympathy with his aspirations, but he still remains frequently ludicrous, buffoonish, and coarse. He need no more be the average Athenian man of the period than Sophocles' Antigone need be the average Athenian girl of the fifth century. We should be very reluctant to accept the caricatures of Aristophanes as average Athenians. I use Aristophanes, like other literary and philosophic writers of the period, only to illuminate religious beliefs and attitudes established by more reliable evidence. Aristophanes is valuable for this purpose, but excessive reliance upon him could lead only to a very distorted picture.

The Athenian poets and philosophers were, of course, aware of the religious attitudes and beliefs of the society in which they lived. In their own writings they were able, as they chose, to adopt, adapt, or combat them. We find authors such as Euripides and Plato taking quite different approaches to popular beliefs at different times, depending on their immediate philosophic and dramatic purposes. The study of the treatment of popular beliefs and attitudes by the literary and philosophic authors will eventually shed some light on popular religion and much light on the methods and purposes of those authors. But one must first, both logically and methodologically, establish independently from these authors what were the popular religious attitudes and beliefs, and that is the purpose of this book.

It is Xenophon alone of the literary figures of the period to whom we must turn as a source for popular religion. He was born ca. 430−425 and came from a family sufficiently prosperous to provide him with the life of a young Athenian aristocrat. In his youth he became acquainted with Socrates, whom he portrays in the *Memorabilia*. Xenophon accompanied the Persian Cyrus in his attempt to seize the kingship, and when Cyrus was killed at Cunaxa and the expedition collapsed in 401, Xenophon helped the ten thousand Greek mercenaries serving Cyrus fight their way from the heart of Persia back to Greek territory. In the *Anabasis* he describes his adventures and successes on this occasion. About 394 he was exiled from Athens for his participation in the expedition of Cyrus, for his support of the Spartan Agesilaus against Athens in the battle of Coronea in 394, or for his generally pro-Spartan sentiments. He settled in Scillus in the Peloponnese and later in Corinth, and he devoted himself to hunting and writing. In his retirement he wrote the *Hellenica*, a history of Greece from 411 to 362, as well as numerous essays on topics ranging from household management to cavalry training.

Xenophon should not be considered a "typical Athenian" of the late fifth and fourth centuries. He clearly lived the life of an aristocrat and was unusually successful militarily and financially. He received some training in philosophy from Socrates and was occasionally classed as a philosopher by the ancients. And, although the Athenians eventually lifted the decree of exile against him, he spent virtually the last half of his life in exile from his homeland.

Despite these factors Xenophon is generally regarded as one of the best sources for popular religious views of the period.[17] His writings are sprinkled with casual and unselfconscious references to religious beliefs and practices, references which lack

any hint of an innovative or polemical outlook. His writings
show him far removed from the intense rationalism of Thucydides, his predecessor in history, and from the intellectual meta-
physics of Plato, his fellow student of Socrates. Nor can he be
likened to the "superstitious man" whom we find caricatured in
Theophrastus (*Char.* 16). He was simply, as Diogenes Laertius
(2.56) characterized him centuries later, "pious, sacrifice-loving,
and able to interpret sacrificial victims." For these reasons his
religious practices and beliefs are very important evidence for
this study.

These are the major ancient sources for Athenian popular religious beliefs, but this study is not confined to them. Others,
ranging from Draco down to the late scholiasts and lexicogra-
phers, are introduced to augment the major sources. But evidence from earlier or later times has been used only to illustrate
beliefs and practices already documented for the late fifth and
fourth centuries.

This is in no sense a general history of Athenian religion,
even within the narrow historical boundaries set. It is rather an
investigation of what might be termed the consensus of popular religious belief, a consensus consisting of those beliefs
which an Athenian citizen thought he could express publicly
and for which he expected to find general acceptance among
his peers. This is only one aspect of Athenian religion in the
period, and it needs to be supplemented by studies of Athenian
deities, festivals, mythology, archaeology and art, and poets,
philosophers, and historians if one wishes to form a comprehensive view of Athenian religion.

T   W   O

Priority of the Divine

If we wish to begin as the Greeks would have, we should begin
with the gods. In innumerable instances the Athenians began
an undertaking, whether a meeting, a war, a literary work, a
personal venture, or an oration, with an invocation, a prayer, or
a statement concerning the gods. Meetings of the ecclesia began with the purificatory sacrifice of a pig and fumigations and
with prayers by the herald.[1] In these meetings the first item on
the agenda concerned "ancestral religious matters," and the
second and third items involved heralds and embassies, individuals who had special status in religious terms because they were
under the protection of the gods. Only after these "religious
items" had been settled were "profane things" introduced.[2]
The members of the boule, the legislative council of five hundred, prayed to Zeus Boulaios and Athena Boulaia as they entered their meeting hall, the bouleuterion (Antiphon 6.45). The
Athenians regularly began the statement of an alliance with a
vow, as in their alliance of 362/1 with the Arcadians and other
Peloponnesian states, in which they promised to Zeus Olympios, Athena Polias, Demeter, Core, the twelve gods, and the
Furies, the so-called "revered goddesses," that they would
make a "sacrifice and a procession" if the results of the alliance
were as they wished.[3] Only after this introductory vow to the
gods were the terms of the alliance given.

Several major speeches opened with prayers. Demosthenes
began *De Corona* (18), the monumental defense of his public

career (in 330), with a prayer that he might receive goodwill and a fair hearing from the jury (18.1–2, 8). The statesman Lycurgus opened his only surviving speech, his prosecution of Leocrates for treason, with a prayer to Athena and the other gods and heroes of the land that he "might be a worthy prosecutor of Leocrates," who had been impious towards them (*Leoc.* 1–2).

Xenophon dared not undertake his momentous excursion with Cyrus until he had first consulted Apollo (*Ana.* 3.1.4–8). It is also Xenophon who announces (*Eq. Mag.* 1.1; cf. 3.1) that the very first task of the cavalry commander is to sacrifice and pray to the gods: only after the gods are "appeased" should one turn his thoughts to the practicalities of recruiting men. After a general introduction and after compliments to his recipient's father, the rhetorician Isocrates begins his essay of moral advice to Demonicus, a young Cyprian, with "be pious in matters concerning the gods, not only by sacrificing but also by remaining true to your oaths."[4] Isocrates then encourages proper behavior towards parents (1.14), which also has a religious sanction,[5] and only then passes on to numerous precepts of a secular nature. Ischomachus, whose discussions with Socrates on household and estate management form the core of Xenophon's *Oeconomicus*, when asked by Socrates to give a complete account of his way of life, begins with his behavior towards the gods (*Oec.* 11.7–8). The same Ischomachus (*Oec.* 7.7–8) began with a prayer the daunting task of educating his wife. Aristotle, when detailing the duties of various Athenian magistrates, describes first their religious duties (*Ath. Pol.* 56.3–5, 57.1–2, 58.1) and only then goes on to detail the secular responsibilities.

Further examples might be introduced, but these are sufficient to demonstrate the broad range of affairs in which priority was given to the gods. As to why the gods had priority, we have no better statement than that made by Demosthenes in the opening of the letter which he wrote to the boule from exile in 323: "I assume that it is proper for a person who is beginning any serious discourse and task to begin first with the gods."[6] It is "proper" in the sense that it "befits" or "suits" the standards of normal conduct. It was the expected thing to do.

When an issue arose which contained both sacred and profane aspects, the Athenian directed his attention first to the sacred. Or, to put it more simply, the gods came first. But were they the most important? Did they maintain this priority in position because their influence in these matters was thought somehow to be greater than that of profane factors? Xenophon, when he saw the soldiers of Agesilaus making religious dedications in Ephesus in 395, asked himself (*Hell.* 3.4.18), "Where men are pious towards the gods, do military exercises, and practise obeying authority, how is it not reasonable that there all things are filled with good expectations?" Does Xenophon, by giving precedence to piety towards the gods, indicate that that is the most important of the three factors? In 343 the orator Aeschines was prosecuted by Demosthenes on charges of treason for sacrificing Athenian interests in negotiations with the Macedonian king Philip concerning the peace of Philocrates of 346. In the peroration of his long and successful defense Aeschines made this plea: "First of all I call upon the gods and implore them to save me, and secondly I implore you the jurors who have the authority to vote in this case to save me" (2.180). Was Aeschines' concern centered first on the gods and only secondarily on the jury?

This is a delicate and complex question. One common scholarly opinion, which derives partly from notions of deterioration of religion in the fourth century, is that these religious statements by orators are only pale and vague mouthings of once-alive religious beliefs: after a nod to jaded religious conventions the orator passed on to the real issues, i.e., the jury, or the evidence, or the arguments of his case. This view is, I think, unduly skeptical and does not properly take into account the frequent recurrence of these "rhetorical" religious expressions in nonoratorical sources such as state and local decrees, dedications, curse tablets, and Xenophon.[7]

The antithetical structure of Greek thought and language

has contributed not a little to a dualistic expression of sacred and profane. Many of these statements are put forward in antithetical μέν . . . δέ clauses, and the conventional priority of the sacred assigns it to the μέν clause. The profane then follows it in the δέ clause. It is also characteristic of this antithetical construction that the speaker gives first, in the μέν clause, the simpler and more familiar element, whereas he reserves for the δέ clause the more complex and immediate element. This allows him to develop or explain without interruption the last idea he has left in the hearers' minds.

The sacred element occurs in this μέν clause not to be dismissed, as is sometimes the case with the content of this clause, but because it is familiar and needs little if any explication. Aeschines (2.180) did not need to detail how the gods were to save him, because the concept was familiar to all his audience. When Demosthenes (18.153) described the events of 339 and 338 in the war against Philip in the following terms, "The Thebans suddenly stopped Philip, most of all, men of Athens, because of the goodwill of some god towards you, but also, so far as one man could influence the events, because of me,"[8] he was not obliged to detail the nature of the "goodwill of some god" towards the Athenians, because this was a familiar concept, but he did require an elaborate demonstration to show his own "influence" on the events of the time. This general familiarity of religious concepts together with the conventional priority of sacred matters naturally assigned the religious statements to the first element of antithetically arranged passages and also naturally meant that they would be rather brief. Another element in the brevity and priority of religious statements is the Athenians' conception of the nature of divine intervention in human life, but this topic will be reserved for later discussion.[9]

In tone and emphasis these dualistic expressions of the sacred and profane remind one of Chaplain Forgy's exhortation to the sailors on the *New Orleans* at Pearl Harbor on 7 December 1941: "Praise the Lord and pass the ammunition." We find a similar juxtaposition of the sacred and general to the profane and specific in military matters in several passages of Xenophon (e.g., *Ana.* 6.5.21). In military affairs the Athenians expressed the first element, "Praise the Lord," through prayers, vows, sacrifices, and a study of the omens,[10] but apart from this, the inclusion of both the sacred and the profane with the emphasis on the need for specific human action has a striking similarity to that modern battle cry. A similar juxtaposition of the sacred and profane with the emphasis on specific human action may be seen in matters of the state as a whole, of legal trials, and of agriculture.[11] The importance of the human action is stated explicitly by Demosthenes (2.23), "A man who is idle himself cannot bid his friends, much less the gods, to do anything on his behalf," and somewhat more philosophically by Ischomachus (Xen. *Oec.* 11.7−8), "I think that I have come to realize that the gods have made it impossible for human beings to prosper without knowing what they must do and without taking care that they do what must be done."

THREE

Areas of Divine Intervention

The gods were thought to intervene and influence human affairs ranging from the state as a whole to the very private concerns of individuals.[1] It will be most convenient first to delineate the areas of this divine intervention and then to discuss in more general terms the nature of the intervention.

It was believed, and especially by Demosthenes, that the gods felt "goodwill" towards Athens.[2] This belief, as Dover suggests, has something of the character of a declaration of faith,[3] and it is nowhere contradicted in our sources. The gods revealed their goodwill by their concern for the general safety and preservation of Athens[4] and by providing to the Athenians opportunities for constructive action in troubled times.[5] This goodwill of the gods led to good fortune, prosperity, and good hopes for the future.[6] It was maintained by upholding oaths, by making the traditional and proper sacrifices, and, at least in Antiphon's view, by freeing the city of any pollution resulting from homicide.[7] The Athenians also tried to maintain this goodwill by consulting the gods, through oracles, when they were uncertain as to the proper handling of religious matters such as portents, festivals, and the disposition of sacred lands and property.[8]

Throughout the late fifth and fourth centuries the Athenians were enmeshed in wars which threatened the welfare of the state as a whole.[9] In this period they endured the loss of the

Peloponnesian War and dissolution of their empire, the civil war between democratic and oligarchic factions, the struggle against Spartan and Theban domination in the early fourth century, and finally the unsuccessful opposition to Philip which ended in Macedonian domination after the battle of Chaeronea in 338. Successes in the battles of these wars were generally credited to the gods, but responsibility for failures tended to be diverted from the gods to a "daimon" or "fortune."[10] Thrasybulus, according to Xenophon (*Hell.* 2.4.14–15), saw the gods providing clear and tangible assistance in the struggle of his democratic faction against the oligarchs in 403 in the civil war:

> The gods are obviously now our allies. In clear weather they create a storm when it is to our advantage, and when we are few attacking many they grant us to set up trophies. And now the gods have brought us to a place where the enemy cannot throw their spears and javelins over the heads of the front ranks because their spears must fly uphill, but we, throwing our spears, javelins, and rocks downhill, will reach them and wound many.

The gods might also make the enemy more vulnerable (Xen. *Ana.* 3.1.22–23) and might grant to the Athenians a general superiority in naval battles (Xen. *Hell.* 7.1.9). With the exception of Thrasybulus' timely storm, there is nothing in the sources which would strike a modern observer as a "supernatural" intervention, and there is no trace of belief in the personal appearance of individual deities or heroes on the battlefield such as we find in the worlds of Homer and Herodotus.[11] In most cases the sources do not describe the specific ways in which the gods influenced the outcome of wars and battles, and one has the impression that on the popular level, Athenians devoted little thought to the mechanics of the matter but were quite content to know that the gods were their allies, allies whose goodwill (Dem. 18.153) functioned in war in the same vague way as it did generally on behalf of the state.[12]

In contrast to the vague notions of how the gods influenced the course of battle stands the strong belief that they had foreknowledge of the outcome of the imminent battle. Xenophon in his essay *On the Cavalry Commander* (9.7–9) provides a concise statement of the Athenian view of the role of the gods in this area:

> If anyone is surprised that many times I have written "Do it with god's help," let him know well that he will be less surprised if he is exposed to danger many times and if he realizes that when war occurs the opponents plot against one another but seldom do they know how their plots are faring. Therefore in such matters one can find no one else with whom to consult except the gods. The gods know all things and in sacrifices, omens, voices, and dreams they give forewarnings to whomever they wish.

The sacrifices and the accompanying study of omens which took place before every battle are based upon this belief.[13] Through sacrifices, study of the entrails, and chance omens such as a sneeze (Xen. *Ana*. 3.2.8–9) the commanders and soldiers received clear signs of the likely success or failure of the forthcoming battle. On one occasion Xenophon and his army of the Ten Thousand, in the face of starvation, delayed three or four critical days solely in the unsuccessful attempt to obtain favorable omens before an attack.[14] Xenophon's serious concern with this, despite great hardships for him and his army, reveals the vitality of the belief in the gods' foreknowledge. This is, however, basically a matter of divination, a topic which is reserved for a separate discussion.[15] A theologian or philosopher would, perhaps, note the possible distinctions between the beliefs that (1) the gods to some extent determine the outcome of battles and war, and (2) the gods have foreknowledge of their outcome. The second belief might well exist without the first, and our sources suggest that the Athenians devoted considerably more thought and attention to the second. But the sources never make a distinction between the two, and the two occasionally appear together with both omens and vows or other "appeasements" of the gods involved (Xen. *Oec.* 5.19–20, *Ana.* 3.2.8–9).

Agriculture was a key element in an ancient economy, and the Athenians believed that humans must serve the gods "for the sake of the produce of the earth, both solid and liquid,[16] and for the sake of their cattle, horses, and sheep" (Xen. *Oec.* 5.19–20). Agricultural success in Greece depends largely upon water of sufficient quantity at the proper times, and it was Zeus who provided this essential water.[17] The god(s) determined the times of the rains as well as their quantity.[18] Even the philosophically minded author of *On the Holy Disease* (1.29–46), an essay on epilepsy, accepted the "divine character" of the occurrence of rain. Aside from the timely provision of water the nature of the intervention of the gods in agriculture is described only in very general terms such as "the good things which the gods provide in their seasons."[19]

The Athenians attempted to maintain divine favor in agricultural matters by the proper performance of traditional sacrifices and festivals (Isoc. 7.29–30), by upholding oaths that included a curse on agricultural produce, by eliminating the pollution of homicide from the city, by harvest festivals (Dem. 21.51–53), and in particular by "first-fruit" offerings.[20] One such first-fruit offering was the *eiresione*, an olive-branch enwrapped with small cakes, loaves of bread, figs, and other fruits of the season. The Athenian placed the *eiresione* at the door of his home and replaced it each year.[21] These first-fruit harvest offerings were very common in all agricultural matters and were based on the belief expressed by Hermogenes in Xenophon's *Symposium* (4.49) that a human being should return to the gods a part of what they gave him. In addition to these practices there were, of course, several religious festivals such as the Thesmophoria and the Eleusinian Mysteries which were directed wholly or in part to agricultural concerns. Famines caused by the anger of an individual deity are familiar from the poetic literature, and two such famines are mentioned in our sources.[22] But these examples are set in mythical times, and there seems in this period to have been little immediate concern with divinely inspired famines.

The concerns of the individual are in part associated with the welfare of the state, and therefore the individual shares in the benefits and the losses which result from divine intervention in matters of the state. But the individual also has concerns quite apart from those of the state as a whole, and he may well have felt the intervention of the gods in these areas more acutely. Xenophon puts into the mouth of Ischomachus (*Oec.* 11.8) a fairly comprehensive list of those matters in which one felt the need of divine assistance in his personal life: "I begin by giving service to the gods and I attempt to act in such a way that it may be right for me, as I pray, to find health, strength of body, honor in the city, goodwill among friends, honorable safety in war, and wealth which is increased honorably." The belief that divine assistance availed the individual in these aspects of his life is not unique to Ischomachus or Xenophon, and reference to most elements of the list can be found elsewhere in our sources.[23]

Strength of body was of great importance to a society engaged in war and farming, and it was no doubt apparent to the Greeks, as it is to us, that this strength results, in varying degrees, both from innate factors and from physical conditioning. We find strength once stressed with no mention of divine help (Xen. *Ana.* 3.1.22–23), but we also find Ischomachus viewing the male's superior strength vis-à-vis the female's as a result of divine structuring of the world (*Oec.* 7.22–31). Strength, like physical beauty (Aeschines 1.133–134), can be the object of prayer (*Oec.* 11.8), and an invalid can attribute his lack of it to a daimon (Lysias 24.21–22).

In matters of health there are two aspects, aspects which might be distinguished as "preventive medicine" and "curative medicine."[24] Preventive medicine took the form of sacrifices and prayers for good health, either by the state on behalf of all its citizens (Dem. 21.51–53; *IG* II² 334) or by one member of a family for other members (Isaeus 8.15–16). In curative medicine the individual turned to a healing god, usually Asclepius in this period.[25] Often the afflicted person would spend the night in Asclepius' sanctuary, either in the city or in the Piraeus. If things went as intended, the god would appear to him in a dream and miraculously cure the disease. The appeal to a healing god often took the form of a vow, a promise to give the god a certain gift if he performed the requested cure.[26] Sometimes vows were taken and dedications erected, usually in the form of statues or columns, by one family member for the healing of his kin.[27] Asclepius occasionally specified to the patient the expected form of repayment. The Athenian woman Rhode was bidden to erect a column (*IG* II^2 4410). Another woman, Ambrosia, had traveled to Asclepius' major cult center in Epidaurus and scoffed at the reports of miraculous cures. Despite this, the god cured her diseased eye, but he ordered her to dedicate, as a memorial of her ill-founded skepticism, a silver pig.[28]

The author of *On the Holy Disease* (1.26–46) lists a number of magical rites and incantations used for the "cure" of epilepsy. Such practices were no doubt common in the treatment of other diseases and would be in full accord with the other behavior of the superstitious man caricatured by Theophrastus (*Char*. 16). The lack of mention of such magic rites in the more public sources suggests that while they may have been privately practised, they to some extent lacked public acceptability. Individuals who mocked the gods or otherwise acted impiously could suffer, from the gods, dreadful physical ailments worse than death (Lysias frag. 73 [Thalheim]) or leading to a painful death (Lysias 6.1–2), but divinely inspired plagues, like divinely inspired famines, seem relegated to the remote past (schol. to Ar. *Lys*. 645).

Since the gods were thought to influence the outcome of battles,[29] we might be surprised to find so few references to prayers and thank-offerings by individuals for "honorable safety in war" (Xen. *Oec*. 11.8). The individual apparently did not perform a personal sacrifice before each battle but let the commanding officers see to this on behalf of the whole army.

After a successful battle the individual may have been content, as a member of the group, with the trophy monuments and magnificent dedications erected by the state or by the generals,[30] and he may have felt little further need to express his personal gratitude. It may be, however, that some of the various weapons and statuettes found in archaeological excavations or recorded on temple inventories were dedications made by individual soldiers.[31]

The acquisition of wealth in the form of money and property, much like success in agriculture, was under the influence of the gods. One could pray for it for the members of one's family (Isaeus 8.15–16), and one could include it in a curse.[32] A grateful mother who had supported her children by her own work might return a portion of it as a first-fruits offering in the form of a statue of Athena, her patroness.[33] The specific nature of divine intervention in this area is never detailed, and the acquisition and preservation of wealth seem generally to fall into the category of good fortune resulting from the goodwill of the gods (Dem. 1.10–11). But lest we think divine influence in this area was too vague to be meaningful, Xenophon, who in 399 had become so impoverished that he had to sell his horse for money for the trip home, heeded a soothsayer's warning that his poverty resulted from neglect of Zeus Meilichios. He quickly sacrificed to Zeus Meilichios, and his financial fortunes took a dramatic and lasting turn for the better (*Ana.* 7.8.1–6).[34]

The two remaining items on Ischomachus' list, "honor in the city" and "goodwill among friends," are of a somewhat different character from the others. They are much less specific and would seem almost to require the simultaneous existence of the other items of the list. We do not find requests for these particular two items expressed so explicitly elsewhere in the sources,[35] although they were surely meant to be included in the more general prayers or wishes for "good fortune." It may have been thought by others that they were the result more of human actions than of divine intervention. It should also be stressed here that Ischomachus' own statement, by its context and phrasing, indicates that all the benefits he catalogues are the result not wholly of divine assistance, but of human actions aided, or at least not hindered, by the gods.

There were important areas of divine intervention in human affairs which Ischomachus did not include in his list, and these concern justice, death, oaths, and divination, each of which will be the subject of a separate discussion. Before treating these, I would like to survey briefly other areas not mentioned by Ischomachus.

Male children were of fundamental importance to Athenian society because as heirs they ensured the continuance of the family and the maintenance of its property and religious cults. It is therefore not surprising to find an Athenian father praying to the gods "that a son be born to him just as a daughter had been."[36] In a particularly strong form of oath, parents might make their children the object of a curse.[37] The gods could thus provide a man with children and, under certain circumstances, could affect the lives of these children.[38]

Apart from the weather that affected war and agriculture the gods were thought also to create the heavy weather at sea that was such a fearful hazard for these seafaring people (Dem. 18.192–194). The risks were so great that when one set out to sea he felt he was virtually entrusting himself to the hands of the gods (Antiphon 5.81–83; Lysias 6.19–20). Andocides, who in 415 had been involved in two of the more blatantly impious acts perpetrated by Athenian citizens, the mutilation of the statues of Hermes and the profanation of the Eleusinian Mysteries,[39] fifteen years later could use his record of safe voyages at sea as proof that he was not an impure and impious man (1.137–139):

> I do not believe that the gods, if they thought they were wronged by me, did not punish me when they had me amidst the greatest dangers. For what danger is greater for men than to sail the sea in wintertime? When they had my person in this situation, when they had control

of my life and property, then were they saving me?[40]
Were they not able even to prevent my body from get-
ting proper burial?

Andocides makes his safety in such perilous circumstances a
proof, if not of divine favor, at least of a lack of divine antagonism towards him. Pleading a similar case, the orator Antiphon
(5.81–83) stresses that the impious man was vulnerable to divine anger in such situations and might well bring destruction
upon his fellow passengers as well as upon himself.

The Gods and Human Justice

Orators, defendants, prosecutors, and jurymen took it for granted that the gods were interested in some aspects of the legal affairs of individual Athenian citizens. The gods' interest and intervention in this area may seem disproportionately great in comparison to their interest in other areas of human life. This may be because of the Athenians' own preoccupation with legal affairs, but also because most of our evidence is drawn from political and forensic orations. A similar disproportion would have resulted if we had necessarily drawn our evidence primarily from sources which treated agriculture or cooking. Essays such as Xenophon's *On the Cavalry Commander* and *Oeconomicus* suggest that nearly every topic of discussion, however prosaic or remote, devoted some considerable time and thought to religious matters. We know more of divine interest in legal affairs because we have more evidence for this area.

The gods involved themselves personally and directly in legal matters of sacrilege such as diverting money owed to a goddess (Dem. 24.121), defacing a temple (Dem. 24.121), and entering a sanctuary when one was polluted (Antiphon 5.81–83). Betraying one's own country was also a form of sacrilege, and the orators assumed that the gods intervened to ensure the punishment of traitors.[1] The gods also punished murderers and perjurors, but these aspects of impiety, together with the divine extralegal punishment of the impious in general, will be discussed later.

The gods played a role in the legal prosecution of individuals on these various charges of impious acts particularly by influencing the mind of the impious person in such a way that he was willing to present himself for trial. In several cases the defendant had returned after a period of absence from Athens, and the prosecutor argues that the gods had put it into the defendant's mind to return so that the Athenian jury would have the opportunity to punish him (Lysias 6.19–20; Lycurgus *Leoc.* 91–92). Some such argument was required, of course, to counter a defendant's claim (Antiphon 5.81–83; Andocides 1.137–139) that his safe sea voyages and general good fortune were clear evidence that the gods were not angry with him. In the trials of individuals charged with treason, murder, or other impious acts the prosecutors also appeal to the gods for inspiration (Lycurgus *Leoc.* 1–2) and threaten the jurors that the guilt for impious acts, like that for murder, falls upon them if they do not properly convict and punish the guilty party.[2]

It would appear that the gods became directly involved in legal affairs only when those affairs concerned (1) acts which were considered impious and (2) perjury. I do not mean here trials for impiety itself, which were quite a different matter,[3] or trials for perjury, which apparently did not exist, but rather legal cases which involved impious acts or perjury. Legal matters outside these two areas could be made the object of a curse,[4] and the defendant might ask the god to give the jurors good sense or might give partial credit to the gods for his past victories and pray for success in the present trial.[5] It was, however, only in cases involving impious acts or perjury that one sensed the immediate and direct intervention of the gods. Andocides, for example, in 415, after he had confessed to participation in the mutilation of the herms, was given immunity from prosecution. Soon afterwards a law was passed forbidding "sinners" to enter public sanctuaries. Andocides returned to Athens in 403, and in 400 was charged with violating the law because he had entered a sanctuary to attend the Eleusinian Mysteries. Leocrates, another example, had fled with his money and concubine from Athens at the news of the defeat at Chaeronea in 338. After staying in Rhodes and Megara for some years he returned to Athens to resume his residency there. In 330 Lycurgus impeached him for treason and brought him to trial. Only in cases such as these were the gods thought to give evidence of guilt or innocence and to serve up the guilty person for trial and punishment.[6] Only in cases involving some form of impiety was it thought that the gods would take cognizance of the vote of each juror and punish him if he voted unjustly.[7]

Only one source suggests that the gods had a real concern with justice beyond matters of impiety and perjury, and that is [Demosthenes] 25, the first speech against Aristogiton. The author claims that "every law is an invention and gift of the gods" (25.16). This is, as Dover notes, a strange statement for Demosthenes to make when he must have been present at the making of some laws.[8] The author also warns that "solemn Justice sits by the throne of Zeus and watches over all the affairs of men" (25.10–11). This is, of course, an idea familiar in poetic literature from Hesiod onwards,[9] but our author uniquely refers the revelation of it to Orpheus. Dover characterizes the idea of personified Justice sitting at Zeus' side as a "fundamental religious concept in the classical period,"[10] but it is surprising that this concept occurs nowhere else in our sources, which are so preoccupied with the problems of human justice on a practical level. [Demosthenes] 25 greatly expands the range of the intervention and interest of the gods in human legal affairs beyond what we find in other sources, and the author implies that the gods were concerned with and active in the establishment and the enforcement of all human law.

I myself believe that this speech was not written by Demosthenes and was never intended to be presented in a law court. It is clearly an imitation of Demosthenic style, and I suspect that it dates from much later than the fourth century. This is not the place to catalogue the stylistic and structural faults of the speech.[11] I simply wish to stress here that it dwells at length upon philosophical and religious discussions which are unparalleled in fourth century forensic and political oratory.[12] The author of this piece knew Demosthenic style, although he made some serious errors of diction, and he knew a fair amount of the story of Aristogiton. What he did not grasp, however, was the nature and content of a fourth-century forensic oration. We may, I think, exclude this speech from our discussion of divine concern for human legal affairs. It is either a late forgery, as I would argue, or at best a statement of idiosyncratic views based on literary and philosophical conceptions which are at variance with the consensus of other sources for popular belief.

It would appear, then, that the gods intervened directly and personally in human legal affairs only when these affairs concerned violations of oaths, murder, treason, or other impious actions. Only in such instances, when their own prerogatives were threatened, did the gods act directly and of their own accord, without human prompting.[13] To this extent the gods showed virtually no concern for the numerous areas of human justice, or even morality, which lay outside these specific areas. Crimes such as theft, embezzlement, assault, rape, and so forth did not concern the gods, unless the crime also included some act of impiety like those detailed above.[14] The numerous and varied literary and philosophical attempts to demonstrate the gods' basic concern for justice and morality seem to have had little positive effect at the popular level. There is abundant evidence from tragedy and comedy that the Athenians knew of some of these literary and philosophical theories and could even appreciate them intellectually, but the evidence here would indicate that no one of these theories had won acceptance or even general recognition in the corpus of popular religious beliefs.

The Gods and Oaths

The violation of an oath was an impious act of the type which the gods were thought to punish.[1] By means of the oath the Athenians involved their gods in a multitude of essentially profane concerns. There is no evidence that lying, cheating, accepting bribes, giving false testimony, intentionally voting unjustly in a law case, and similar "wrongs" were thought in themselves to be of concern to the gods. But the Athenians loaded these wrongs, together with a host of others, with religious content when they made them the object of promissory oaths. When the individual had previously sworn not to do something, such as the taking of a bribe, if he then committed that act, he made himself liable not only to prosecution for the illegal act but also to divine punishment for breaking his oath. Divine punishment would befall him not because of the illegal act *per se*, but only because he had violated his promissory oath when he committed that act.

A very full and detailed example of such promissory oaths is that sworn by the jurors at the beginning of their year of service:

> "I will vote in accordance with the laws and decrees of
> the Athenian people and of the boule of five hundred.
> And I will not vote to have a tyrant or an oligarchy. If
> someone attempts to destroy the power of the Athenian
> people or if he speaks or brings a vote contrary to this, I

will not be persuaded. Nor will I vote for the cancellation
of private debts or for the redistribution of Athenian
land or houses. I will not bring back those who have
been exiled or condemned to death. I will not myself
banish, nor will I allow anyone else to banish, the resi-
dents here contrary to the established laws and decrees of
the Athenian people and boule. And I will not confirm
in office a person in such a way that he holds one office
when he is subject to audit for another, and these offices
include the nine archons, the hieromnemon,[2] those who
are chosen by lot with the nine archons on this day, a
herald, an embassy, and delegates to the council of allies.
Nor will I allow the same man to hold the same office
twice or the same man to hold two offices in the same
year. And I will not accept bribes because of my jury
service, not I myself nor another for me nor in any other
way with me knowing of it, not by a trick or by any
contrivance. And I am not less than thirty years old. And
I will listen to both the prosecutor and the defendant
equally, and I will bring my vote on the basis of the issues being prosecuted." The juror is to swear by Zeus,
Poseidon, and Demeter, and he is to curse himself and
his family to utter destruction if he transgresses any of
these things, but he is to pray that if he keeps his oath
there may be many good things for him.[3]

(Dem. 24.149–151)

No one of the acts described in this juror's oath was considered
pious or impious in itself; but through the oath, the Athenians
cast over them all, for those who took the oath, the additional
shield of divine protection. The doing of a forbidden deed then
automatically meant violation of the oath, and this violation invited divine punishment.

In such promissory oaths the Athenians presupposed, or at
least implied, that the gods were aware or could make themselves aware of individual acts by individual human beings. The
gods must also have been thought to be familiar with the more

or less conventional standards of human morality if they were to judge the upholding or violation of certain provisions of these oaths. The oath of the members of the boule to "counsel the best things for the city" (Lysias 31.1–2) and even more so the solemn oath of the archons that "they will rule justly" (Arist. *Ath. Pol.* 55.5) presuppose that the gods knew the standards by which such matters could be judged. The gods knew the thoughts as well as the acts of individuals, and thus these promissory oaths could include a provision against thinking one thing but saying another (Dinarchus 1.46–47; Dem. 18.282).

Lycurgus (*Leoc.* 79) reveals the importance of such promissory oaths when he claims that "it is the oath which holds together the democracy. For there are three elements of which the government consists, the archon, the juryman, and the private citizen. Each of these gives a pledge [consisting of an oath]." We have already seen the juror's oath. The archons twice swore, once on a sacred rock near the marketplace and once on the Acropolis, that they would rule justly and in accordance with the laws. They pledged not to take bribes and, if they did so, to erect a golden statue.[4] By the oath of the "private citizen," Lycurgus no doubt meant the oath which an Athenian young man swore in the sanctuary of the goddess Aglaurus at some time in his two years of military and religious training:

> I will not bring shame upon these sacred weapons nor
> will I abandon my comrade-in-arms wherever I stand in
> the ranks. I will defend both the holy and profane things.
> I will not hand on the fatherland smaller than I received
> it, but larger and better, so far as it lies in my power with
> the assistance of all the other citizens. I will obey the
> officials who govern wisely and the laws, both those
> which are already established and those which are wisely
> established in the future. If anyone attempts to destroy
> them, I will not allow it, so far as it lies in my power
> with the assistance of all the other citizens. I will hold in
> honor the ancestral sanctuaries. The following gods are

> witnesses: Aglaurus, Hestia, Enyo, Enyalius, Ares and Athena Areia, Zeus, Thallo, Auxo, Hegemone, Heracles, the territory of the fatherland, the wheat, barley, vines, olive-trees, and fig-trees.[5]

These promissory oaths raised the proper performance of a citizen's duties above the level of the profane and made them an object of divine concern. Evidently the Athenians themselves, no less than some modern scholars, were aware of the basic amorality of the gods and by means of the oath virtually coerced the gods to become involved in these affairs of human morality. In theoretical terms their involvement was only secondary; that is, it was limited to punishing the violation of the oath. In practical terms this theoretical distinction did not matter, because, for example, if a juror accepted a bribe, he broke his oath and was liable to divine punishment, and this prospect could serve as a deterrent.

In most of the instances already described a legal sanction against the performance of the deed accompanied the divine sanction against the violation of the oath. Where a legal sanction did not exist the whole weight lay upon the divine one. Such was the situation for the speech-writer Lysias. In 404 he and his family were caught up in the Thirty Tyrants' attempt to arrest foreigners resident in Athens and to confiscate their property. Lysias attempted to escape by bribing the agent sent to arrest him. Since no conventional legal sanctions were available to him, all Lysias could do was to put the agent under oath and have him "invoke utter destruction upon himself and his children" in case he violated their agreement (12.9–10). But it was primarily in international dealings that legal sanctions were lacking, and in this area oaths were widely used. They were sworn to strengthen the resolve to undertake common ventures,[6] and they were often the only sanction available when opposing generals came to terms on the battlefield.[7] Oaths were, of course, at least from Homer's time onward a regular feature of treaties and alliances.

It would be difficult to overstate the frequency with which oaths were employed in the affairs of individuals. We find, for example, fathers and other members of the group using the oath to attest to the proper qualifications of a young man for membership in the deme, the phratry, and the genos.[8] In each of these cases the oath is taken to guarantee the truth of the statements made, and this, for the individual, was surely the most common use of the oath. With an oath a father denies that an individual is his son (Andocides 1.126), a woman declares knowledge of a financial transaction (Lysias 32.13), a prosecutor attests to the facts of his case (Dem. 54.40–41), and witnesses declare the truth of their testimony (Arist. *Ath. Pol.* 55.5; Xen. *Ap.* 24). Unusually strong oaths were required at every stage of trials for murder, because it was thought particularly important that in such cases the truth be known.[9]

The individual often specified in a curse the punishment which should afflict him if he violated his oath. A very full and elaborate form of such a curse is that which the Athenians along with other members of the international council supervising Delphi swore in the early sixth century concerning the sacred land. The orator Aeschines treats the provisions and curses of this oath as still effective in the mid-fourth century (3.108–111):

> If any city, private citizen, or race violates these provisions, let that city, private citizen, or race be under the curse of Apollo, Artemis, Leto, and Athena Pronaia. And the curse is upon them that their land not bear produce, and that their wives bear offspring not like their parents, but monstrosities, that their cattle not produce offspring in the normal way, that they suffer defeat in war and in legal cases and in the marketplace, and that they themselves be completely destroyed together with their houses and race. And, it says, may they never sacrifice in a holy way to Apollo, Artemis, Leto, and Athena Pronaia, and may these deities not receive the sacrifices which they make.[10]

This unusually comprehensive form of oath touches upon most of the areas in which the gods were thought to intervene in human affairs. In the less elaborate oaths of individuals the curse is usually limited to the destruction of one's self and one's family.[11]

Every oath implied a curse on the violator whether or not the curse was expressly detailed. Since it was acknowledged that the gods punished the perjuror in some way, the taking of an oath by itself subjected the individual to some form of punishment if he violated his oath. The addition of a curse only specified the area in which it was to fall. The punishment would occur with or without the curse, but the curse added more weight to the oath by specifying that the punishment not concern relatively trivial matters but those objects of greatest importance to the individual. It should be noted that in many cases our sources report that someone took an oath but do not record the actual words. In most of these cases the oath would have included a more or less specific curse.

The addition of curses to oaths presupposes that the gods punished those who committed perjury. The primary punishment was, of course, the fulfilment of the curse which was explicit or implicit in the oath. But in addition, violation of an oath was an act of impiety which could disturb in more general terms the good relationship between men and gods, and thus it could affect the general prosperity, the gods' willingness to help in war, and one's own "good hopes" for the future.[12]

The Athenians believed that the children and family of a perjuror might be punished.[13] This belief is a particular instance of a principle which in earlier times was much more widely applied, that is, that the family as a group bears a collective responsibility for the misbehavior of the individual members of the family.[14] In the fourth century the application of this principle in religious matters concerned mostly, though not exclusively, the destruction of the family and children of the individual who violates his oath.[15] The survival of this principle here may be due in part to the almost formulaic inclusion, going back as far as Homer, of family and children among the objects of curses.

The orators stress the omniscience and omnipotence of the gods in their enforcement of oaths. Lycurgus (*Leoc.* 79) puts it succinctly: "No one who has committed perjury can escape the notice of the gods or escape punishment from them." Xenophon (*Ana.* 2.5.5–7) expresses it somewhat more dramatically through the mouth of his comrade, the Spartan Clearchus: "I could never deem happy a man who is aware that he has disregarded such oaths. For I do not know with what swiftness of foot he might escape the hostility of the gods or any place to which he might flee, nor do I know any dark spot he might run off to or how he might withdraw to a secure place. For all things everywhere are subject to the gods and they control all things equally." The common practice of taking oaths in sanctuaries may reflect not so much doubt of the omniscience of the gods as a desire to increase the solemnity of the occasion.[16]

Our sources appear to present a highly idealized picture of contemporary beliefs concerning oaths. If there were throughout the society a strong and uniform belief in the efficacy of the oath and of divine punishment for perjury—as the oratorical sources would have us believe—the situation would be like that which Plato (*Lg.* 12.948B–D) attributes to the mythical age of the Cretan king Rhadamanthys:

> Rhadamanthys saw that men in his time clearly believed in the gods, and with good reason, since many men at that time were descendants of the gods, like Rhadamanthys himself, as we are told. Evidently he thought that lawsuits should not be entrusted to a human being to decide, but to gods, and as a result lawsuits were judged simply and quickly by him. By giving to the litigants an oath concerning each of the disputed points he reconciled them quickly and surely.

In such an age intentional perjury would be unthinkable, and all legal disputes could be justly settled by putting the disputants under oath. The Athenians of the fourth century, of course, did not do this, but rather used oaths as just one of several elements in building their legal cases.[17] The majority vote, whether in law cases or in deciding membership in a group, prevailed over the oath of an individual.[18] The Athenians

clearly believed that individuals might on occasion intentionally commit perjury. Plato (*Lg.* 12.948B–D) attributes abuse of
the oath to three causes: "Some men do not believe in the gods
at all and some think the gods have no concern about us. Others, those who are most numerous and most wicked, are of the
opinion that if the gods receive flattery and some small sacrifices they help us steal a lot of money and rescue us from great
punishments."[19] Xenophon (*Mem.* 1.1.19), in his praise of Socrates' fidelity to his oaths, implies that not all people believed
the gods were omniscient in matters concerning oaths.[20]

In a private and practical way the Athenians may have enter-
tained doubts about the efficacy of oaths and of divine punishment for perjury, but it was clearly not fashionable to express
these sentiments in a public forum. The maintenance of oaths
was in fact considered a key element of piety. When Xenophon
(*Ages.* 3.1–5) has promised us a description of the piety of his
friend Agesilaus, he treats *only* Agesilaus' maintenance of his
oaths. In other sources the maintenance of oaths is clearly a
part of piety,[21] but it is usually stressed by being given particular prominence or by being set slightly apart from the more
general notion of piety.[22] Despite the individuals' personal reservations, the public upholding of the efficacy of the oath was
of major importance for the ethical structure of the society, because it was only through the oath that a significant proportion
of an individual's private and civic activities was brought under
religious sanctions.[23]

S I X

Divination

"The gods know all things and in sacrifices, omens, voices, and dreams they give forewarnings to whomever they wish." In these few words Xenophon (*Eq. Mag.* 9.7–9) expresses the belief which resulted in numerous and varied practices of divination.[1] There may have been some skepticism about the omniscience of the gods (Xen. *Mem.* 1.1.19, *Symp.* 4.47–49), but the belief that they gave to men signs concerning the future seems to have been almost unanimously accepted. Xenophon lists "sacrifices, omens, voices, and dreams" as the means by which the gods give these signs, and there are several instances of the use of each of these in our sources.[2] Xenophon's claim that the gods "give forewarnings to whomever they wish" and, by implication, not necessarily to everyone, is confirmed elsewhere. Demosthenes (19.297–299) and Aeschines (3.130) both view it as an indication of divine concern for Athens that certain oracles about military and political affairs had been given to the Athenians.[3] Lycurgus (*Leoc.* 93) makes the point explicitly in his account of the punishment of Callistratus, an Athenian orator who in 361 was condemned to death:

> What old man does not remember or what young man has not heard of Callistratus, the man whom the city condemned to death? He went into exile, and after he heard from the god in Delphi that if he came back to Athens he would find just treatment from the laws, he

returned and took refuge at the altar of the twelve gods. But nonetheless he was put to death by the city, and justly too. For just treatment from the laws for criminals is punishment. And the god rightly gave to the victims the opportunity to punish the guilty man. For it would be terrible if the same divine signs appeared to the pious and to the wicked.

There appears in our sources no questioning of this belief that "the gods know all things and in sacrifices, omens, voices, and dreams they give forewarnings to whomever they wish."[4] The few reservations about divination concern dreams.[5] Twice (Hyperides 4.15–16 [Kenyon]; Aeschines 3.77) it is alleged that a prophetic dream was misrepresented by a human agent, but the belief that a god might send a prophetic dream to a human being is not called into question. Plato (*Lg*. 10.909E–910A) and Theophrastus (*Char*. 16.4) both criticize the manner in which superstitious people react to dreams, and these philosophers might well have questioned the divine origin of dreams in general. Skepticism concerning the reliability of dreams may have arisen in part because of the acknowledged difficulty of properly interpreting the dream (Xen. *Ana*. 3.1.11–12),[6] but mostly, it would seem, because of a doubt concerning the credibility of the recipient.

Laymen could interpret their dreams, oracles, or signs in sacrifices on their own, but quite often they turned to professionals for assistance. These professionals included chresmologues ("speakers" or "collectors" of oracles) and manteis (soothsayers). Chresmologues provided to their clients, whether the state or individuals, oracles attributed to authorities such as Apollo, Orpheus, and Musaeus, and then interpreted them to suit the immediate occasion. In the late fifth century some of these "oracle-mongers" such as Lampon enjoyed considerable notoriety, prosperity, and even recognition by the state, but in 413, when their influential predictions of Athenian success in the Sicilian expedition proved so disastrously wrong, the chresmologues suffered the ire of the public and virtually disappeared from sight.[7] A mantis, by contrast, combined inspiration from a god with technical knowledge of divination and could thereby prophesy, interpret oracles, and explain the significance of dreams and omens. Manteis continued to work and prosper throughout the fourth century. Both as private citizen and as military commander, Xenophon regularly turned to them for assistance in explaining dreams, omens, and signs in sacrifices.[8] These manteis were often foreigners who moved from city to city as business demanded. Isocrates (19.5–7) tells of Thrasyllus of Aegina, who retired to his homeland after amassing a large fortune as an itinerant mantis. And in 394/3 the Athenians awarded Sthorys of Thasus citizenship and pay for his assistance in their victory in the sea battle at Cnidus against the Spartan forces.[9] To the successful Thrasyllus and Sthorys we might contrast "the manteis and vagabond priests" who, as Plato complains, went about knocking on the doors of the wealthy looking for business.[10]

For interpretations not of omens and oracles but of certain aspects of sacred law the individual could turn to an exegete, an "interpreter" or "expounder." In contrast to the often non-Athenian, itinerant manteis, exegetes were Athenian citizens serving as public officials. They had special knowledge of sacred law, and although there is considerable uncertainty as to their precise duties, we do know that in the fourth century they described the law and its prescriptions to individuals who consulted them on special problems, particularly problems concerning the pollution of death and the ritual of burial.[11]

Exegetes escaped criticism of their work, but Aristophanes (e.g., *Pax* 1043–1126, *Av.* 959–991) and his fellow comic poets of the mid- to late fifth century mocked chresmologues and manteis.[12] These criticisms appear directed at the exotic oracles and pretensions of individuals rather than at divination itself or at the oracles from respected sources such as Delphi. We should note that even Plato, who sought reform of so many contemporary religious practices, repeatedly reveals his own trust in the pronouncements of the Delphic oracle.[13]

The Athenians used prophecy, naturally, to obtain some information in those areas which lay beyond human comprehension. In his ideal city Plato (*Rep.* 4.427B–C) leaves to Apollo of Delphi the foundings of sanctuaries, sacrifices, and the other services of the god and the dead, because, as Socrates says, "we ourselves do not understand such things." Xenophon (*Eq. Mag.* 9.7–9) stresses the importance of the god's help in war because "when war occurs the opponents plot against one another, but seldom do they know how their plots are faring. Therefore in such matters one can find no one else with whom to consult except the gods." In very general terms divination and divine signs concerned incidents and aspects of life which lay beyond human knowledge and control. The extent to which the Athenians practised divination might, therefore, be viewed as an index of their own estimation of their rational understanding of the world about them. In those areas in which they felt confidence in their own abilities they acted on their own, but in those areas of life in which they thought their own understanding deficient they practiced divination.

A survey of the uses of divination reveals that the majority of them concerned religious questions and that the Athenians, like Plato himself, thought it best to let the gods decide such problems. Most innovations or changes in matters of cult required divine sanction, in the form of either command or approval. The state could be ordered by Delphi or Zeus' oracle at Dodona to institute new festivals or sacrifices, and the decision to introduce new cults might be subject to oracular approval.[14] When the Athenians were troubled by a bad portent ([Dem.] 43.66; Aeschines 3.130) or by a religious oversight (Dem. 21.51–53; Arist. *Ath. Pol.* 54.6–8), the oracle was consulted and recommended new festivals and sacrifices as a means to rectify these problems. Changes involving the property of the gods, such as the decision to cultivate a portion of sacred land (*IG* II² 204, lines 23–54) or to build a new altar (*SEG* 21, no. 519, lines 1–17), also required divine approval. The establishment of a new priest (*IG* II² 4969) might also be subject to oracular consultation. An individual too might be motivated by an oracle (*IG* II² 4602), a dream (*IG* IV² 121, lines 33–41; Plato *Lg.* 10.909E–910A), or an omen (Theophrastus *Char.* 16.4) to erect a dedication, an altar, or even a sanctuary.

In the complex polytheistic system of the Athenians the various gods had different though occasionally overlapping functions, and the question often arose which god should be invoked or appeased in a given situation. Just such a question faced Xenophon when he was invited to join the expedition of Cyrus in 401. In making this major decision Xenophon turned to Delphi, and his account of this (*Ana.* 3.1.4–8) not only presents a typical instance of divination but also reveals one of its difficulties: how to phrase the question so as to gain the information you desire.

> There was in the army a man named Xenophon, an Athenian, and he was following along although he was neither a general nor a captain nor a soldier. Proxenus, an old friend from abroad, had sent for him from his home and promised him that if he did come he would make him a friend of Cyrus. . . . After Xenophon had read the letter he consulted Socrates the Athenian about the expedition. Socrates suspected that the city might view it as a criminal act if Xenophon became Cyrus' friend, because Cyrus appeared eagerly to be assisting the Lacedaemonians in their war against Athens. Therefore Socrates advised Xenophon to go to Delphi and consult the god about the expedition. Xenophon went and asked Apollo to which of the gods he should sacrifice and pray so that he might in the best possible way make the journey which he had in mind and so that after good success he might return safely. Apollo told him in reply the gods to whom he ought to sacrifice.
>
> When Xenophon returned to Athens he told Socrates of the oracular response. And when Socrates had heard he chided Xenophon because he did not first ask the god whether it was better for him to go on the expedition or to remain at home, but instead, after he had himself decided he must go, he asked the god how he might do this in the best way. "But since you asked in that way," Socrates said, "you must do what the god commanded." And Xenophon, after he had sacrificed to the gods whom

Apollo bid, set sail, and he overtook Proxenus and Cyrus in Sardis when they were about to start the journey inland, and he met Cyrus.

Like Xenophon, the state and other individuals turned to an oracle when they were unsure which god had jurisdiction in a certain matter (Xen. *Vect.* 6.2–3; [Dem.] 43.66; Theophrastus *Char.* 16).

The procedure for a state enquiry at an oracle was often elaborate and required considerable expense and delay. A detailed example of these procedures is the enquiry the state made in 352/1 concerning the cultivation and rental of some sacred land in the deme Eleusis (*IG* II² 204, lines 23–54):

The secretary of the boule is to write onto two equal and identical plates of tin as follows: onto the one, "If it is more agreeable and better for the Athenian people that the archon rent out the currently cultivated parts of the sacred land which lie within the boundaries to raise funds for the building of the stoa and for repair of the sanctuary of the two goddesses." And onto the other tin plate he is to write, "If it is more agreeable and better for the Athenian people to leave the currently cultivated parts of the sacred land within the boundaries untilled for the two goddesses." And when the secretary does inscribe them, let the overseer of the presiding officers take and roll up each tin plate and after he has wrapped them in wool let him cast them into a bronze pitcher in the presence of the people. And let the prytanists[15] make these preparations and let the treasurers of the goddess deliver to the people immediately a gold and a silver pitcher. And let the overseer shake the bronze pitcher and draw out in turn each tin tablet, and let him cast the first one into the gold pitcher and the second one into the silver pitcher, and let him close up the pitchers. And let the overseer of the prytanists seal them with the public seal, and let whoever wishes of the other Athenians also seal them. And when they are sealed let the treasurers carry the pitchers up into the Acropolis.

And let the people choose three men, one from the
boule and two from all the Athenians, men who will go
to Delphi and will ask the god which of the two inscribed tablets the Athenians should follow in their actions concerning the sacred land, whether the one from
the gold pitcher or the one from the silver pitcher. And
when they have come back from the god let them take
down the pitchers and let be read to the people the oracle and the inscriptions from the tin tablets. And they are
to act in accordance with this inscribed tablet which the
god says it is more agreeable and better for the Athenian
people to follow. And they are to do this so that things
concerning the two goddesses may be as pious as possible and so that in the future no impiety may ever occur
concerning the sacred land and the other sanctuaries in
Athens.[16]

The elaborate precautions to determine Apollo's will were
made "so that things concerning the two goddesses might be as
pious as possible and so that in the future no impiety may ever
occur concerning the sacred land and other sanctuaries in
Athens." The concern that the intended action be "pious," i.e.,
acceptable to the gods, was always the reason for consulting oracles in religious matters, but it was so obvious to all that it was
not usually explicitly stated.[17]

In situations of war the Athenians also turned to divination
for guidance. Xenophon (*Eq. Mag.* 9.7–9) stresses the limits of
human knowledge in war and attributes to this the need to
consult the gods. Xenophon himself did this regularly, and
with the aid of dreams, omens, sacrifices, and oracles he made
all the major decisions which concerned him personally and his
army.[18] One should not assume that Xenophon was more zeal-
ous in this than his contemporaries.[19] Uniquely in the literature
of the period the *Anabasis* presents the memoirs of a soldier
and general in the field, and it is because of its unique form that
the *Anabasis* provides such an intimate account of the everyday
details, including those of divination, of military life. The relative lack of descriptions of divination in other sources describ-

ing military campaigns does not indicate that it was not being practised, but only that the authors, since they were not writing personal memoirs, did not deem these details worthy of description. It should be noted that Xenophon gives no indication that his fellow officers or his men, despite occasional personal inconvenience, thought his dependence on divination excessive or eccentric. There are criticisms of military leaders of this period or slightly earlier for excessive dependence on divination, but these criticisms stem either from intellectual sources such as Thucydides or from late authors like Plutarch.[20] We find no such criticisms in our sources for popular religious beliefs.

Divination was used primarily in matters concerning religion and war. It is only Theophrastus' superstitious man (*Char.* 16) whose life is affected daily, even hourly, by omens, portents, and dreams:

> The superstitious man is the kind of person who during the day would walk around only after he had washed his hands and sprinkled himself [in the Enneacrounos][21] and after he had taken into his mouth a bit of laurel from the sanctuary. If a weasel runs across the road,[22] he does not proceed until someone else goes by or until he throws three stones across the road. And if he sees a snake in his house, if it is a reddish-brown one, he calls upon Sabazius,[23] but if it is a holy one,[24] he immediately builds a sanctuary on the spot. And as he passes by the shining stones at the forks in the road he pours olive-oil on them from his flask, and he leaves only after he has fallen to his knees and done obeisance. If a mouse eats through a sack of his barley-meal, he goes to the exegete[25] to ask what he ought to do. If the exegete tells him to give the sack to a saddler to stitch up, he does not heed this advice but goes away and performs expiations. And he is apt to clean his house constantly because, as he says, someone invoked Hecate against it. If owls hoot at him as he is walking along, he is thrown into a dither and continues

on only after he has said, "Athena is mightier." And he
does not step on a tomb, nor is he willing to pay his
respects to a dead man or to a woman after childbirth.
He says that it is better for him not to become polluted.

On the fourth and seventh days of the month[26] he orders the boiling of wine for the household, and he goes
out to buy myrtle, frankincense, and sacrificial cakes.
When he returns he spends the whole day placing gar-
lands on the hermaphrodites and sacrificing. And when
he has a dream he goes to the dream-interpreters, to the
soothsayers, and the bird-watchers to ask to which
god or goddess he ought to pray. He goes each month
with his wife to the Orpheotelestae[27] to be initiated, but
if his wife doesn't have the time he goes with the nurse
and children.

And he would seem to be one of those who carefully
sprinkle themselves at the sea. And if he ever sees that
one [of the statues of Hecate] at the forks in the road has
been garlanded with garlic,[28] he goes off to wash himself
from head to toe, and after summoning priestesses he
orders them to purify him with a squill or a puppy. And
if he sees a madman or an epileptic he shudders and spits
into his pocket.

The superstitious man views every trivial occurrence—a weasel
crossing his path or the hoot of an owl—as a sign from the
gods and spends much of his life reacting to these signs. Theophrastus defines superstition as "a kind of cowardice towards
the divine": the superstitious man interprets the various trivial
events of everyday life as signs of immediate or impending danger. The orator Antiphon (5.81–83) also associates divine signs
with "dangerous" affairs of state and with the "dangers" of sea
travel, and it was no doubt the dangers as well as the uncertain-
ties which motivated the extensive use of divination in time of
war. We must not let Theophrastus' caricature stand as a model
of the average Athenian of the fourth century, but the superstitious man's unusually great cowardice is revealing.[29] Other

Athenians, like him, turned to divination in situations where there was danger of impiety or, as in war, a danger of personal suffering, but they were less fearful than he.

It appears from the forensic orations which survive that when speaking before an Athenian jury, an Athenian avoided representing himself as dependent upon or even as very concerned with divination in his personal life. Nowhere does an Athenian litigant claim that an oracle, omen, or prophet motivated or had any influence upon his actions. Clearly divine signs, except in cases involving impiety,[30] were irrelevant to legal responsibility. They were not even introduced as ameliorating circumstances. Either Athenians of the period did not regularly practise divination in their personal lives outside of matters of grave physical danger and religious uncertainty, or such practices lacked, to a certain extent, public respectability and acceptance. To judge from Xenophon, Aristophanes, Theophrastus, and other sources, some Athenians did regularly practise divination in their daily lives, and therefore we must conclude that the divination of individuals in personal matters, as contrasted to that practised by the state in public matters, to some extent lacked general acceptance and public respectability.

The Athenians did not use divination simply to gain a revelation of the future in a casual or curious way.[31] Nearly all its uses, except perhaps some of those of Theophrastus' superstitious man, were associated with specific acts which were being planned or undertaken. A common form of enquiry was, "Is it more agreeable and better to . . . ?"[32] The state or individual was simply asking if it was more beneficial to do, or not to do, the proposed act (Xen. *Mem.* 1.1.2–3).[33] Divine help was not requested, nor was the nature of the benefit specified. In some situations, such as immediately before a battle, the benefit might be obvious, but in most cases it was not. The benefit might be something quite unexpected, as when, after Xenophon's sacrifices proved unfavorable for battle, one soldier (mistakenly, however) reported that a fleet was on its way to rescue the army (*Ana.* 6.14.12–22). For the most part, however, it seems that the Athenians were content with learning only if "things would be more agreeable and better" in the future if they did the proposed act.[34] Disregarding an unfavorable omen resulted in suffering, perhaps because of divine punishment (Xen. *Symp.* 4.47–49), but mostly because one had chosen what was more unpleasant and worse.[35] It was, of course, impossible to prove an oracle right or wrong when the question was put into the form "Is it more agreeable and better to . . . ?" The unspecific nature of the questions may be one reason why the oracles maintained their credibility in some circles until late antiquity.

The Gods and Death

The gods whose intervention in other areas of human life has been described were thought to have little or no influence on the time or nature of an individual's death. The gods could, of course, cause diseases (Lysias 6.1–2 and frag. 73 [Thalheim]) and hazards at sea (Antiphon 5.81–83; Andocides 1.137–139), and these might well result in death. But in the descriptions of such cases the speakers have their attention focused on the god's punishment of individuals for impious acts, and the stress is upon the sufferings of the individuals while they are alive, not upon their deaths. When death itself is the subject of discussion, the gods are absent. It is rather fortune, a daimon, or destiny which is held responsible for an individual's death.[1] This is a manifestation of the prevailing tendency to assign unpleasant events not to the gods but to fortune or a daimon.[2] Our sources indicate that popular belief, like most of the literary treatments, kept the gods apart from all matters of death.[3] The orator at the state funeral of the Athenian soldiers who died in 338 at Chaeronea thought, in fact, that it was improper even to mention the name of Dionysus on such an occasion ([Dem.] 60.30).

Homicide, however, whether intentional or unintentional, was thought to bring into play supernatural forces. There were two quite distinct religious aspects of murder, that of pollution and that of avenging spirits.[4] Antiphon in the *Tetralogies* provides the fullest and most vivid description of the "avenging spirits" in a hypothetical speech by a prosecutor (4.1.2–4).[5]

When god, wishing to create the human race, begot the first of us he gave to us as nurturers and helpers the earth and the sea so that we might not die from a lack of the necessities before the natural end in old age. Because god so valued life, whoever illegally kills someone commits an impious act against the gods and throws into confusion the customs of men. The one who has died, since he is deprived of those things which the god gave him, naturally leaves behind as the vengeance of god the hostility of the avenging spirits. Those who unjustly judge the case or unjustly testify, by joining in the impiety of the one doing these things, bring this hostility of the avenging spirits, a defilement which was not originally theirs, into their own houses. And if we, while professedly seeking vengeance for the dead, should prosecute innocent men because of some personal hatred, we will have as terrible avenging spirits against us the avengers of the dead for whom we have not sought vengeance. And if we unjustly put to death guiltless men we are subject to the penalties for murder, and by persuading you to act illegally we become responsible for your sin.[6]

The victim left behind spirits to take vengeance on the murderer. These spirits were filled with "wrath" and "hostility" towards the murderer, but beyond that we are told nothing of how they expressed this wrath or how they exacted their vengeance. These spirits of vengeance afflicted primarily the murderer, but they could also fall upon anyone who thwarted the proper prosecution and punishment of the murderer. They thus could attack the jurors or even the prosecutors.

In the sources for popular religion we find these avenging spirits of homicide victims only in Antiphon's *Tetralogies*. These *Tetralogies* are somewhat earlier than our other sources and were not intended to be delivered to a jury or a legislative assembly. It would appear that in the fourth century Antiphon's wrathful spirits were no longer believed to be active forces in matters of homicide. Their *floruit* had been in the past, a past which Aeschylus conjures up in his treatment of avenging spirits in the *Oresteia*. Plato (*Lg.* 9.865D–E) calls his own description of similar spirits "a venerable old story."[7] Vengeance for the victim was still believed necessary, but it was entrusted to human, not supernatural, agents.[8]

Everywhere else in our sources, including other speeches of Antiphon, the dominant religious concern in matters of homicide was pollution. The murderer committed an impious deed and brought upon himself the pollution of bloodshed. This pollution was, as it were, contagious and could afflict innocent persons who came into contact with the murderer. It could even afflict the whole city and cause dearths and ill-fortune.[9] Because of his impiety, but even more because of the contagious character of his pollution, the murderer was excluded by law "from the water of purification, from libations, from the wine-bowls, from the sanctuaries," and from "sacrifices and contests." The murderer was also barred, because of his pollution, from the marketplace and the city itself.[10] According to Antiphon (2.3.9–11, 3.3.11–12) this pollution might also be transferred to the jurors and prosecutors who did not properly prosecute and punish the murderer.

The concept of the murderer's pollution remained very much alive in the fourth century. This may be because it had been institutionalized in Draco's law code of the late seventh century (Dem. 20.158), and therefore prohibitions based on this concept of pollution continued to be enforced although the belief in pollution itself may have weakened. The sources of the period stress the importance of law and tradition in these matters and do not treat the evils of the pollution itself.[11] One senses that their attention centers more on the institution than on the actual pollution. The institutionalizing of the prohibitions may be one reason why in cases of homicide the prohibitions based on the belief in pollution continued to be enforced although belief in avenging spirits and wrathful, active souls of homicide victims, a belief upon which the belief in pollution was at least partly based, had largely disappeared.[12]

The Nature of Divine Intervention

Although the Athenians had rather specific beliefs about the areas of human life in which the gods intervened, they seem to have been content, on the popular level, with only the vaguest notions about the nature and mechanical operation of this intervention. The sources would suggest that with some notable exceptions, the Athenians had little feeling of immediacy concerning the gods' involvement in their affairs. Divine intervention was usually several steps, or causes, removed from the event or situation under consideration. The persistent concern with maintaining or winning "the goodwill of the gods" illustrates this point. The goodwill of the gods was essential for the prosperity of the state and individual, and from it came good fortune, safety, good hopes for the future, opportunities, and success in war, financial matters, and divination. This goodwill was maintained primarily by upholding oaths and by duly performing the proper and traditional sacrifices. But nowhere is interest shown in how this divine goodwill operated in the realm of human affairs.[1] It is simply there, or if it is not, it must be reestablished. It lies very much in the background of events and situations and its place in a chain of causality is never specified, but however remote and indefinite it may be, human success is impossible without it.

Even more remote in the chain of causality was a primordial structuring of nature for which Xenophon in particular sees the god(s) responsible. In the *Oeconomicus*, which is a philosophically oriented didactic essay, Xenophon assigns to "the god" the credit for having established the relationships between the human sexes (7.22–31):

> Since both the indoor and outdoor tasks require work and attention, the god straightway prepared, as it seems to me, the soul of the woman for the indoor work and concerns but the soul of the man for the outdoor work. He made the body and soul of the man more able to endure cold and heat and journeys and military expeditions, and as a result he assigned to him the outdoor work. And because for the woman he made the body less able to withstand these things he assigned to her, I think, the indoor work. And knowing that he had created in her and had assigned to her the sustenance of the newborn children, he also dispensed more affection for newborn babies to her than he did to the man. And since the god had assigned to the woman the protection of the stores, knowing that for such protection a fearful soul is no disadvantage, he dispensed more fear to the woman than to the man. And because he knew that if anyone wronged the family the one handling the outdoor work would have to come to the defense, he dispensed more courage to the man. But because it is necessary for both to give and receive money, he put down memory and diligence equally for each to claim, and therefore you cannot determine whether the male or the female sex has the advantage in these. And the god put down proper self-control equally for each to claim, and he gave to whichever one is better, the man or the woman, permission to win a greater share of this good.
>
> Because the natures of both are not well suited for all the same things, the two have a greater need of one another and the two become more beneficial to each other, the one having the abilities the other lacks. Knowing these things, we each must try to accomplish as best we can the proper things which have been assigned to each

of us by the god. The law, which unites man and woman, also advises these things, and just as the god made man and woman partners for children, so the law makes them partners for the family. And in addition the law shows that those things in which the god has made each of the two more capable are good, for it is better for a woman to remain indoors than to take care of matters outdoors. And if someone acts contrary to the ways established by the god perhaps his disorderly behavior is seen by the gods and he pays a penalty for neglecting his own work or for doing his wife's work.

In a similar vein, but in a different work, Xenophon claims that "gods gave to mankind the ability to teach a human being by words what he ought to do" and that "the mane, forelock, and tail were given to horses by the gods for the purpose of decoration" (*Eq.* 8.13, 5.8). There is the strong likelihood that in assigning responsibility for the structuring of nature to the gods in this way Xenophon was reaching beyond popular conceptions of divine activity. In our sources, besides Xenophon, only Antiphon, a philosopher and sophist, in the third *Tetralogy* (4.1.2–4) reflects the belief that the god(s) were the architects of the world as we know it.

The most immediate examples of divine intervention are those found in the cult of the healing god Asclepius. This immediacy is suggested by the experience which Ambrosia, an Athenian woman, had at his sanctuary in Epidaurus (*IG* IV² 121, lines 33–41):

Ambrosia from Athens, blind in one eye. She came as a suppliant to Asclepius. As she walked about in the sanctuary she laughed at some of the cures, thinking it unbelievable and impossible, that, for example, the lame and blind became well merely by having a dream. But when she went to sleep she had a dream. The god seemed to stand over her and say that he would make her healthy, but in repayment she must erect in the sanctuary a silver pig as a memorial of her folly. And after the god had said this he seemed to tear open her diseased eye and to pour in some drug. And when day came Ambrosia went out healthy.

Even simpler, more humble dedications such as the following one of a woman named Rhode (*IG* II² 4410) reveal the directness of Asclepius' intervention.[2]

> As the god commanded her
> Rhode [erected this column] for Asclepius
> in the priesthood of
> Olympichus of the deme Kydathenaion.

The immediacy felt in this god's intervention may result from the tangible character of what was sought from him, i.e., the cure of a specific medical problem, but it was also the natural result of the operation of his cult.[3] Many of the miraculous healings were accomplished while the patients slept in the sanctuary, either through dreams revealing prescriptions and regimens for health or through miraculous "medical" treatments by the god himself. Thus immediacy was inherent both in the nature of the affliction and in the operation of the cult.[4]

If we judge from our sources, the Athenians sensed an immediacy of divine intervention to this extent only in a few other areas such as the provision of rain for agriculture and protection from the dangers of seafaring.[5] The gods also intervened directly in human life through giving omens, voices, and dreams,[6] but this was passive rather than active, since in matters which did not directly concern cult, men elicited information from the gods about future benefits of planned actions, but the gods did not on their own initiative intervene to guide or manipulate human action through these prophetic signs.

Most divine intervention lay between these extremes of structuring nature and of direct action in the present. It was thought, again in a rather vague and ill-defined way, that the gods could affect or influence the minds of individual men. In 346 Isocrates wrote an open letter to Philip urging him to assume the leadership of a Panhellenic expedition against the king of Persia. In the course of this letter Isocrates (5.150–151) suggests that "perhaps" the gods gave him his own rhetorical ability.[7] In the same passage he claims that the gods "do not with their own hands create the goods and evils which befall men, but they create in each man a state of mind of such a type that goods and evils come into being for us through one another." This is the clearest statement we have of the mechanical operation by which the gods intervened in human life. Lycurgus (*Leoc.* 91–92) also describes the gods' influence on an individual's rational faculties, but he limits this influence to "leading astray" or "bewitching" the mind of an individual such as Leocrates who has offended the gods by an impious act.[8] The gods punish the person by affecting his mind so that he will do acts which lead to his punishment on the human level.[9] In just this way Androtion, who was accused of stealing money belonging to Athena (Dem. 24.121), and the impious Andocides (Lysias 6.19–20) were brought to trial. And thus, apart from Isocrates' bit of self-conceit about his divinely apportioned rhetorical ability, the detailed instances of divine influence on the human mind concern only cases in which the gods are punishing impious individuals.

Prayers often expressed the wish that the gods affect the mind of the speaker or of the audience in a favorable way. Xenophon opens his essay on the cavalry commander with the injunction, "You ought to sacrifice and to ask the gods to grant that you think, say, and do those things from which you might hold your office in a way most pleasing to the gods and in a way most dear, most glorious, and most beneficial to yourself, your friends, and your city" (*Eq. Mag.* 1.1). Ischomachus prayed that he "might teach" and his wife "might learn the things that were best for both" of them (*Oec.* 7.7–8). Demosthenes prayed that "it might come into [his] mind to write and into the minds of those Athenians in the ecclesia to choose what is best now and in the future for the Athenian people" (*Epist.* 1.1).[10] And in *De Corona* Demosthenes twice prays that the jurors have towards him "the same goodwill" which he had towards the city (18.1–2, 8). He concludes this speech with a prayer to the gods that they put into his enemies "better reason and better thoughts" (18.324).[11] Behind all these statements, both those describing the punishment of the impious and those asking for positive mental conditions, lies the belief that the gods can and do affect the minds of individual men.[12] But as so often, the descriptions of the good things which the gods can bestow in this area are vague and general, but the descriptions of the punishment of impious malefactors are specific and gripping. One is therefore inclined, perhaps wrongly, to assume that a stronger belief underlay the latter than the former.

Related to the idea that gods could affect men's minds, but on the ethical rather than on the purely rational level, is the belief that they could make men's souls "better." Xenophon expresses this belief in contexts of warfare, when he claims that his men "by the gods' help," had better souls than the Persians,[13] and when he describes how a god could inspire "virtue," i.e., courage, into men (*Hell.* 7.4.32). Xenophon alone among our sources describes divine intervention in this area, and even he, in the *Oeconomicus* (7.22–31), puts forward the quite different thought that while the god assigns various virtues to men and women, the attainment of these virtues depends to a certain extent upon the individual himself.

The gods were thought to reveal their goodwill by providing men opportunities for action. Orators speaking before the ecclesia drew upon this belief to designate an alliance which they favored as an opportunity provided by the gods.[14] Prosecutors in law cases claimed that the gods gave the Athenian people the opportunity to punish impious criminals.[15] In this area, too, the means by which the gods provided opportunities are not specified, and the intervention of the gods is several stages removed from the final act. Human beings are given full latitude either to seize these opportunities or to let them pass by.

In the great majority of cases a speaker assigns to "the gods" responsibility only for what is, in the speaker's view, good and desirable. We have seen the gods given at least partial credit for the general safety and preservation of the state, for its good fortune, prosperity, and good hopes for the future, for success in war and agriculture, and for an individual's health, strength of body, honor in the city, goodwill among friends, wealth, children, and safety in war and at sea. But who or what was responsible for failure in these areas? One cause, frequently mentioned by Demosthenes, who was himself obliged to explain a number of "failures," was that men had not made use of the opportunities provided by the gods (1.10–11). But more commonly it was a daimon or fortune which received the responsibility for failure or for any result which was, in the eyes of the speaker, unfavorable.[16] Demosthenes' explanation of the Athenian defeat in the battle of Chaeronea (18.192–194) is an interesting example of this type of reasoning:

> At that time some of the terrible things were in the future, as it seemed, but some were already at hand. Consider what was my policy for the government in these circumstances. Do not maliciously attack the results of it, because the outcome of all things is as the daimon wishes it. But the policy itself reveals the intent of the adviser. Do not reckon it my crime if Philip happened to win the battle. The outcome of this was in the god's power, not in mine. But show me that I did not choose all those things which were possible so far as human calculation can go, and that I did not do these things honestly and carefully and with an effort even beyond my powers. Show me that I did not initiate actions that were good, necessary, and worthy of the city. Show me that, and then bring prosecution against me.
>
> But if the resulting storm overcame not only us but all the other Greeks, what must be done? It is as if someone accused a shipowner of causing a shipwreck after the shipowner had done everything for safety's sake, after he had provided the boat with all the equipment he thought might save it, but then suffered a storm in which his equipment was damaged or even completely destroyed. "But I was not piloting the boat," he might say. So too I

was not even a general. And the shipowner might also say, "I did not control fortune, but fortune controls all things." [17]

Demosthenes believed that he had done everything humanly possible, that he had seized every opportunity, but still the battle had been lost. He makes the familiar point that the outcome of battle was in the god's hands, and to this extent he would seem to be imputing the blame to a god. But he precedes this remark with a statement that "the outcome of all things is as the daimon wishes it," and in the simile concluding the passage he attributes such unhappy results to "fortune." In this passage "the daimon," "the god," and "fortune" seem to merge into one force,[18] and as elsewhere in Demosthenes responsibility for failure is deflected from the gods to a daimon or fortune. In a similar manner Demosthenes attributes Philip's success to fortune (2.22) and Aeschines blames Alexander's obliteration of Thebes in 335 on a "daimonic force" (3.133). And elsewhere failure in those areas in which the gods can grant success is attributed to a daimon or fortune.[19] The gods give strength of body, but an invalid places responsibility for his condition on a daimon (Lysias 24.21–22). The gods, at least in Aristophanes, can grant old age, but fortune or a daimon is responsible for untimely death.[20] And death in general, when described from a sympathetic point of view, is always attributed to a daimon, fortune, or destiny, never to the gods.

The negative aspect of fortune, that is, "ill-fortune" as described above, was not a religious concept insofar as ill-fortune was not a deity to whom prayer and worship were directed. Ill-fortune had no cult, but did serve as a convenient explanation, if not as the only cause, of various unpleasantries of life. From a theological point of view the opposition between the gods who give "good things" and ill-fortune which gives "bad things" is noteworthy, but there is no indication in our sources of any theological or philosophical basis to this antithesis. The antithesis appears simplistic and naive, but it was clearly acceptable at the popular level.

There was, however, a positive side to fortune, "good fortune," and in the third century and later this formed the foundation of an important religious cult in Athens and elsewhere. Fortune (τύχη) and good fortune (ἀγαθὴ τύχη) eventually became major cult figures with temples, festivals, sacrifices, and dedications.[21] There are signs of the beginnings of this development in the fourth century.[22] In this period some of the functions customarily assigned to the gods were occasionally attributed to fortune alone. A number of things which were, in the speaker's estimation, favorable were now occasionally ascribed to fortune rather than to the gods. The Athenians, for example, claimed that their earliest ancestor Erechtheus (or Erichthonius) had been born from the soil of Attica itself. As his descendants they prided themselves on never having "immigrated," in contrast in particular to several Dorian peoples. Isocrates (4.26) describes this cherished "autochthony" of the Athenians as a gift of fortune. Demosthenes quite often speaks of the assistance given by fortune to Athens in her war against Philip.[23] Even the successes of Philip, when described by his partisan, may be ascribed to fortune as well as to the gods (Isoc. 5.152). Xenophon, who elsewhere speaks little of fortune, once mentions the role which fortune played as a "general" in determining the strategy of the Ten Thousand (*Ana*. 2.2.13). In personal affairs also, fortune is occasionally given a role usually reserved for the gods. Lysias (13.63) credits fortune with the rescue of men who were facing certain death, and an individual might thank fortune for the preservation of his money (Dem. 1.10–11, 43.67). And, finally, criminals might be brought to trial by fortune (Lysias 12.80; Aeschines 2.183; Dinarchus 1.29, 98). But here there is an important distinction between the workings of fortune and of the gods. The gods intervened to effect the legal punishment only of those who engaged in impious activities,[24] whereas fortune acted against those engaged in nonreligious crimes.

These occasional and scattered attributions to fortune of duties customarily assigned to the gods are harbingers of the future development and importance of a cult of Fortune.[25] The sources, however, do not treat fortune as a deity to whom one renders worship. There was, by 335/4, a state cult of Good Fortune ('Αγαθὴ Τύχη) with the usual apparatus and personnel of established cults.[26] But there is no indication that our sources, in their occasional references to fortune (τύχη) or good fortune (εὐτυχία), have this or any other specific deity in mind.[27] In the fourth century fortune still appears to be, for our sources, a secular notion. Fortune seems to be primarily "the course of events,"[28] or "the way things turn out," but the tendency to explain by fortune events once attributed to the gods lays the conceptual foundation for the later development of fortune as a religious figure.

In order to conclude this examination of the nature of divine intervention it is necessary to recall the previous discussions concerning the priority of the divine and dualistic expressions of the type "First of all I call upon the gods and implore them to save me, and secondly I implore you the jurors . . . to save me" (Aeschines 2.180).[29] In such dualistic expressions and in nearly all longer treatments of divine intervention the gods are assigned only partial responsibility for the act, result, or situation under consideration. Full responsibility seems to fall upon them only in those few areas in which their intervention was felt to be most "immediate," as in healing and the provision of rain. But usually divine intervention was more remote, and in these cases the popular conception was, generally, that humans must act upon the opportunities which the goodwill of the gods provided. The Athenians troubled themselves little as to how this goodwill functioned, but they recognized that it was essential for human success. But even when the goodwill of the gods was assured, and even in those areas in which the gods were thought to intervene, ultimate success or failure depended heavily upon the actions of the men themselves.[30] In simple terms, opportunities came from the gods. It was up to the human being to make the best of them. If he was successful, he praised and thanked the gods. If he failed, he faulted, if not himself, a daimon or fortune.

The Nature of the Gods

In the previous chapters the areas and nature of the intervention of "the gods" have been examined. But who were these
gods? To those familiar with ancient Greek literature the answer would seem obvious: they were Zeus, Hera, Athena,
Apollo, and the other gods and goddesses of the Homeric pantheon. This answer, in fact, may be correct, but here, where
our preconceptions are so strong, we must be particularly care-
ful to note how the Athenians expressed their beliefs concerning "the gods."

When an Athenian spoke of intervention of "the gods," he
meant intervention by gods and goddesses as distinct from heroes and from divine forces of the vengeful and hostile type.
Heroes were human beings, often like king Theseus major figures of the mythological past, who after their deaths received
cults and worship at their tombs.[1] The Athenians commonly
distinguished between "gods" and these "heroes," and there is
no indication in our sources that the Athenians classed the heroes among "the gods."[2]

Isocrates (5.117) also makes a distinction between the Olympian gods who were the cause of good things and other deities
who were responsible for misfortunes and vengeance:

> Those gods who are the cause of good things for us are
> called "Olympian," but those who have been assigned to
> misfortunes and vengeance have epithets which are more

> unpleasant. Private citizens and states erect temples and
> altars of the Olympians. Those other gods are not hon-
> ored in prayers or sacrifices, but rather we perform rites
> to get rid of them.

Individuals prayed, sacrificed, and erected temples and altars to
the Olympians, but sought only to avert the others. One such
malevolent deity was, at one time, the avenging spirit which
afflicted the murderer.[3] Isocrates' distinction between Olympian gods and malevolent deities is not identical with the
much-discussed distinction between "Olympian" or "heavenly"
deities and "chthonic" deities.[4] Plato (*Lg.* 4.717A, 8.828A–C)
recommends that the features of the worship and cult of the
heavenly and chthonic deities be kept separate. This prescrip-
tive, and perhaps overly schematic,[5] statement refers only to
cult practices and does not necessarily define either the nature
or the functions of the deities. Apart from Plato our sources
take little notice of the distinction. A deity is termed chthonic
only when his function in the underworld is stressed and he
might be confused with a deity of the same name who has
functions in the upper world. On the lead curse tablets Hermes
and Hecate are given the epithets Chthonicus and Chthonius,[6]
and these serve to specify their underworld role on this occasion and to distinguish them from their counterparts in the upper world. The use of these epithets, like the analogous use of
Katochos ("Holder-down" or "Spellbinder") on the tablets,[7] is
perfectly understandable and does not indicate any general
classification of deities.

"The gods," as referred to by our sources, probably included
some chthonic as well as purely Olympian deities. The Zeus
Meilichios to whom Xenophon sacrificed, with notable success, in order to restore his depleted financial resources (*Ana.*
7.8.1–6) was certainly chthonic,[8] and Demeter was at least partially so. They both, I think, would have been included among
"the gods." The more important distinction, in popular belief,
was between the gods who give what is good and the various

vengeful and hostile forces which can cause what is unpleasant and undesirable.

The popular conception of a daimon and of its relationship to the gods appears to have been quite vague and imprecise. Plato distinguishes clearly between gods and daimons and alone among our sources leaves the impression that a daimon might have a cult in the form of a sanctuary and sacrifices.[9] A similar but less explicit distinction between gods and daimons is apparent also in the several sources, discussed previously, which assign to the gods credit for human success but to a daimon the responsibility for misfortunes, failure, and death. There was also in the Greek religious and literary tradition a concept of daimon which equated daimons and gods rather than distinguished between them. In Homer, for example, if a character believed that he had witnessed an instance of divine intervention but was unable at the moment to name the specific god responsible, he often attributed the intervention to a daimon. The poet then usually revealed the identity of the god, and in this manner the daimon and the god were equated.[10] In much the same manner Isocrates, urging pious behavior on the Cyprian Demonicus, uses "the gods" and "the daimonic [element]" synonymously (1.12–13):

> First, be pious in matters concerning the gods, not only by sacrificing but also by remaining true to your oaths. The former is an indication of a ready supply of money, but the latter is an indication of goodness of character. Always honor the daimonic [element], but especially in association with your city. For thus you will seem at the same time to be sacrificing and to be following the laws of the city.

Demosthenes also on one occasion (18.192–194) uses "the gods" and "the daimon" almost interchangeably[11] and he can amplify "the gods" with the phrase "and the daimonic [element]" (19.239–240). In the middle of the fourth century the famous courtesan Phryne, in the aftermath of a lovers' quarrel, was charged with impiety for introducing a new "god" into Athens.[12] Fifty years earlier Socrates had been tried for introducing new "daimonic powers" (Xen. *Mem.* 1.1.2–3; Diogenes L. 2.40). The accusation against both was clearly the same, but for Socrates the phrase "new daimonic powers" was probably inserted in place of "new gods" because it was commonly known that Socrates spoke of his inner prophetic voice as a "daimonion" ("little daimon"), and not as a god (Xen. *Mem.* 1.1.2–3).[13] Each of these instances indicates some equation of gods and daimons, but most often gods and daimons were distinguished in the sense that the gods were given credit for successes while the daimons were held responsible for failures.

Except for occasional hints in Plato there is no evidence for any cult associated with daimons in this period. They, as distinct from the gods, had no sanctuaries, and they received no sacrifices or prayers or rites of aversion. To this extent, like fortune, they were not religious figures. They existed largely, I suspect, because of the Athenians' reluctance to hold "the gods" responsible for misfortunes, failure, and death. The daimons provided, conceptually if not in cult, the supernatural sanction for the unpleasant side of life.[14]

The conclusion is, thus far, that when the Athenians spoke of "the gods" they did not include under this title the heroes, daimons, or the various minor malevolent and vengeful divine forces.

In the sources most references concerning the divine world are simply to "the gods," and these references far outnumber those to specific deities. It is in large part this tendency to refer to the gods in a general and collective manner, rather than individually and specifically, which has convinced some scholars that religious belief in this period was degenerate and a mere shadow of what it had once been.[15]

We must note, however, that in some cases where a speaker or author refers to "the gods" or "the god" he has in mind specific gods. For example, when Xenophon bids his countrymen "to ask the gods" if they should accept his proposals for economic reform (*Vect.* 6.2–3), he means Zeus of Dodona and Apollo of Delphi. An Athenian speaker nearly always means one or both of these gods when he is discussing oracles. When a speaker refers to "the god" sending rain he means Zeus.[16] In the law-courts speakers often told the jurors that "the gods" would punish them if they violated their oath.[17] It is probable that here they meant Zeus, Poseidon, and Demeter, the gods by whom the jurors had sworn (Dem. 24.149–151). It may even be that generally when punishment from the gods is threatened for perjury the speaker assumes that the specific gods invoked in the curse will act, but just as the words of the curse itself and the names of the gods are often not given, so too the author speaks only in general terms of "the gods" and does not name the particular gods involved.

But even if we eliminate all instances in which the speaker may possibly have had in mind specific gods, there remain a very large number of references simply to "the gods." From the previous discussions it is generally clear which group of gods and goddesses was meant by this term, but, beyond that, there is no specification of name, epithet, attributes, place of residence, or physical and psychological characteristics. The term "the gods" is, as it were, an abstract collective,[18] and the persistent conception of the divine in this abstract and collective manner is one of the features which, although not unique to popular religion, tends to distinguish it from its literary counterpart.

Outside the context of cult practice, this collective of the gods is homogeneous. "The gods" are not divided into individuals or factions, and the opposition of one god or of one faction of gods to another, an opposition so important in epic and drama, seems alien to the popular conception of the divine.

This abstract and collective conception of the gods may be seen more clearly in the usage of the term "the god" and the relationship of "the god" to "the gods."[19] Xenophon in the *Oeconomicus* (7.22–31) and Antiphon in the third *Tetralogy* (4.1.2–4, 4.2.7) attribute to "the god" the structuring of nature.[20] In the battle of Mantinea of 362, which most thought would decide the leadership of the Greek world between the Spartans and Thebans, both sides claimed victory but neither established dominance. Xenophon (*Hell.* 7.5.26) attributed this unexpected result to "the god." The speechwriter Lysias (6.19–20) speaks of "the god" who punishes impious wrongdoers, and Demosthenes (18.192–194) attributes the loss of the battle of Chaeronea, in part, to "the god." [21] In each of these cases the author does not specify "the god" by name, and it would be wrong, I think, to allow our preconceptions developed from poetic literature to prevail and to assume that this "god" was Zeus. There are indications that the authors were using "the god" in the same way they elsewhere used "the gods," i.e., to designate the abstract and unified collective of divine powers. Xenophon in the *Oeconomicus* (7.22–31) speaks of "the god" structuring nature, but elsewhere in the *Oeconomicus* (7.18–19, 10.7) and in his essay on horsemanship (*Eq.* 5.6, 5.8, 8.13) he attributes this same structuring of nature to "the gods." Lysias (6.19–20) speaks of "the god" who will punish Andocides, while Andocides, in reply to the same point, talks of "the gods" who punish impious men (1.137–139). We have here not different conceptions concerning the same religious point, with, for example, Lysias believing that one god punishes the impious and Andocides believing that several gods do this. We have rather two different ways, "the gods" and "the god," of referring to the same abstract and unified collective of divine forces. [22]

The most common term for this collective was clearly "the gods," but the occasional use of "the god" was understandable to an Athenian audience. And it is not surprising that it was, for the practice is attested throughout the Greek religious and literary tradition from Homer onwards. [23]

This abstract conception of a homogeneous collective of the gods prevailed only outside the framework of cult. In cult practices such as prayers, sacrifices, and dedications the full multiplicity of a polytheistic system appears. Erchia was, for example, only one of 139 demes in Attica, but on its calendar of public sacrifices forty-three individual deities and heroes are listed as recipients of sacrifices in the course of one year.[24] In this deme Apollo and Zeus each have six different epithets. At least thirty-five separate cult sites, some probably consisting of only an altar, are specified. Hermes and the "Heroines" each had two separate sanctuaries within the deme. There would also have been deities, sacrifices, and cult sites in Erchia which did not fall into the compass of this calendar. The calendar lists only those annual sacrifices in whose financing the deme as a whole was involved, and there would have been biennial and quadrennial sacrifices as well as sacrifices of family groups and private associations which were not recorded here. The large number of deities and cult sites listed is not peculiar to the deme Erchia. Other sacred calendars and various other sources indicate that a similar number and variety of deities and cult sites existed throughout Attica.[25]

The god Zeus provides a good though perhaps extreme illustration of the complexity and multiplicity of the polytheistic system. In the sources for our period Zeus has numerous different epithets, and to greater or lesser degrees each of these epithets indicates a different god with distinct functions and cult centers. The six epithets recorded for Zeus on the sacred calendar of Erchia (Epakrios, Epopetes, Horios, Meilichios, Polieus, and Teleios) each distinguish a separate Zeus with his own cult center and sacrifices.[26] The functions of Zeus Epakrios ("Zeus on the Heights") and of Zeus Epopetes ("Zeus the Overseer") are unknown, although the first may be associated with Zeus' common function of providing rain.[27] Zeus Horios ("Zeus of the Boundaries") was responsible for the preservation of boundary stones, while Zeus Teleios, affiliated with Hera, attended to marriage.[28] Zeus Polieus ("Zeus of the City"), like Athena Polias, was concerned with the welfare of the polis, i.e., of the city-state, or in this context, perhaps of the political unit of the deme. The Zeus Meilichios ("Zeus the Kindly") to whom both the Erchians and Xenophon (*Ana.* 7.8.1–6) sacrificed is no doubt the same god, although the sites of the sacrifices and the victims differed. The partially "wine-less" character of the Erchian sacrifices and Xenophon's complete burning of the victim are both characteristic of offerings to the chthonic type of deity which this god represents.[29] The occasion for each sacrifice was different: the Erchians made their sacrifice as a regular part of their program of annual sacrifices; Xenophon performed a special sacrifice to accomplish a specific purpose. But nonetheless, the same god was the recipient of both sacrifices.

In Athenian cults outside of the deme Erchia, Zeus Boulaios was, together with Athena Boulaia, the patron deity of the boule, and Zeus Phratrios oversaw the activities of the phratry.[30] Each phratry had its own Zeus Phratrios and its own cult center apart from the state cult of Zeus Phratrios.[31] Zeus Boulaios and Zeus Phratrios existed and functioned only within the framework of their respective religious and political organizations. Zeus Herkeios ("Zeus of the Fence") and Zeus Ktesios ("Zeus of the Stores") were each associated with a slightly different aspect of family life.[32] Zeus Herkeios had an altar in the courtyard of the house and protected its perimeter. Zeus Ktesios was represented by a jar, or by "tokens" affixed to a jar, in the storeroom. Isaeus (8.15–16) provides us with a charming and rare description of one type of family sacrifice and prayers directed to this Zeus:

> We have also other proofs that we are the sons of the daughter of Ciron. For as was natural, since we were children of his own daughter, Ciron never made any sacrifice without us, but whether his sacrifices were large or small we were always present there and we sacrificed with him. And not only were we invited to such things, but he always used to take us to the countryside to the festival of Dionysus, and we used to sit at his side and watch, and we celebrated all the festivals with him. And when he sacrificed to Zeus Ktesios he was especially serious about the sacrifice, and he did not admit any slaves or freeborn illegitimate children, but he performed all the rites by himself. We shared in this sacrifice and we lent a hand in performing the rites and we with him put

offerings on the altar and we assisted in doing the other things. And Ciron used to pray to Zeus Ktesios to give good health and good property[33] to us, and this was only natural because he was our grandfather.

Zeus Hypatos ("Zeus the Highest") had an altar at the entrance of the Erechtheum on the Acropolis (Paus. 1.26.5), and together with Heracles and Apollo Prostaterios he received state sacrifices and prayers "for health" (Dem. 21.51–53). Apollo also bade the Athenians to sacrifice to him after an unfavorable portent ([Dem.] 43.66). Zeus Olympios, whose sanctuary was the Olympieum, was invoked by Demosthenes (24.121) and, together with other deities, received from the Athenian people a promise of a sacrifice and a procession if an alliance turned out to be beneficial (IG II[2] 112). The eponymous archon superintended the annual procession for Zeus Soter ("Zeus the Savior") (Arist. Ath. Pol. 56.3–5), whose cult was centered in the stoa of Zeus.[34] Zeus Soter was credited with "saving" the Athenians from slavery in the Persian Wars.[35] Xenophon attributed to this same god an omen promising "safety" in a military campaign (Ana. 3.2.8–9). The cult of Zeus Basileus ("Zeus the King"), whom Apollo bade Xenophon to honor during his expedition with Cyrus (Ana. 3.1.4–8, 3.1.11–12, 6.1.20–24), was situated in a stoa in the marketplace.[36]

Zeus Naios of Dodona provided numerous oracles to the Athenians when they were suspicious of Delphi's political motivations.[37] The Zeus who provided rain was commonly mentioned without an epithet.[38] A Zeus without an epithet is also made a witness of the oath of jurors,[39] and was claimed by Demosthenes to have sent him a dream announcing the death of Philip (Aeschines 3.77). The epithets of the Zeuses who received dedications like that of Nicagora (IG II[2] 4602) would have been apparent from the sanctuary in which the dedication was originally placed.[40]

Each of the Zeuses specified by an epithet is to a greater or lesser degree a separate deity. Each received sacrifices at different times and different places, and occasionally the sacrifices were of a quite different character. Each Zeus had a different function, although as with Zeus Herkeios and Zeus Ktesios these functions may have occasionally overlapped. The sphere of influence of different Zeuses, as for instance of Zeus Boulaios, Zeus Ktesios, and Zeus Phratrios, was often centered on different social and political units. That all these individual deities were called Zeus is a result of the development of Greek religion in much earlier periods; in practical terms, in the fourth century these various Zeuses were treated, particularly in cult, as different, independent deities.[41]

In our sources there is no trace of an attempt to anthropomorphize these Zeuses. There are no descriptions of their physical or psychological characteristics. Such anthropomorphism as did occur, outside literary and mythical treatments, is probably to be found in the iconography of their sanctuaries. There were cult statues of some of them, and dedications may also have portrayed them. But it would appear from our sources that the anthropomorphic conceptions which were developed in literature and art played a very minor role in the everyday consideration of these deities. Our sources are concerned, primarily and almost exclusively, with their function, not with their physical and psychological characteristics.

What has been said above, by way of example, concerning Zeus can be applied equally well to Apollo, Athena, and the other gods, goddesses, and heroes of the Athenian pantheon. For purposes of cult, for sacrifices, prayers, and dedications, and in matters of specific need the Athenians made use of a large number of individual deities, each of whom had his own cult site, his own sacrifices, and his own functions. These functions overlapped considerably, and Athenians in different areas of Attica, or in the context of different social groups, often appealed to different gods to achieve essentially the same purpose.

The appeal to a large number of particularized gods in cult settings and the conception of an undifferentiated collective of gods in a noncult setting is a paradox of Athenian popular religious belief. The origins of this paradox, like the origins of the many Zeuses, must lie in the development of Greek religion in earlier periods. But however it came about, this paradox is a distinguishing feature of Athenian popular religion.

The Afterlife

The Athenians' views concerning the afterlife show more variety and uncertainty than their views on any other religious topic.[1] Differing beliefs are expressed explicitly or implicitly on such fundamental questions as whether the soul continued to exist, where the souls of the dead resided, whether the souls had perception of the life of the living, and whether the souls encountered rewards and punishments in the afterlife.

Most Attic epitaphs of this period say nothing about the afterlife. They rather, like the following two epitaphs, list the individual's virtues in this life, lament his death, and describe the sorrow of his relatives.[2]

> Philostratus, son of Philoxenus,
> Your father's father's name you bore,
> But to your parents "Chatterbox,"
> Once their joy, now mourned by all,
> By a daimon you were carried off.
>
> (Peek, *GV* no. 1499 = *IG* II² 12974)

> Had you, by fortune's escort, attained maturity,
> We all foresaw in you, Macareus, a great man,
> A master of the tragic art among the Greeks.
> But now, in death, your reputation does remain
>   For temperance and virtue.
>
> (Peek, *GV* no. 1698 = *IG* II² 6626)

Such epitaphs need not be taken to demonstrate that the Athenians did not believe in an afterlife, but they do indicate, as do other sources, that Athenian popular religion was focused almost exclusively on life in this world, not in the next.[3] Those epitaphs which do mention the afterlife speak in vague terms of the soul being with Persephone and Pluto, as in the following:

> Your virtue left behind many monuments,
> In Greece and in the minds of men,
> Of the kind of man you were, Nicobolus,
> When, mourned by friends, you left the sun's bright light
> And descended to the house of Persephone.
> (Peek, *GV* no. 1492 = *IG* II² 6004)

> It is an easy thing to praise good men.
> Abundant eulogies are quickly found.
> Now, in the chamber of Persephone,
>   The chamber shared by all,
> You, Dionysius, enjoy such praise.
> Your body, Dionysius, lies here,
> But your immortal soul is now possessed
>   By the dispenser shared by all.
> In death you left behind undying grief
> For your friends, your mother, and your sisters.
> (Peek, *GV* no. 1889 = *IG* II² 11169)

The house and chamber of Persephone[4] and Pluto had been, of course, familiar features of the underworld since Homer, but Attic epitaphs of the fourth century describe none of the other literary features of the underworld such as the river Acheron, the ferryman Charon, or the dog Cerberus. The references to Persephone and Pluto in these epitaphs may be merely reflections of a poetic tradition with little or no basis in contemporary religious belief.[5]

The soul of the deceased supposedly traveled from the upper world to the house of Persephone, and it was the function of Hermes Psychopompos ("Hermes the Escorter of Souls") to guide the souls on this journey.[6] It is this belief which is implicit in the practice of burying curse tablets in graves. On these crudely inscribed lead tablets were written curses, often against opponents in legal proceedings. About three hundred have been found in Attica and published. The following two, dating from early to mid-fourth century B.C., reflect the general nature of these tablets:

> I put under a spell to Hermes Katochos[7] and Persephone Litias,[8] the tongue of Litias, the hands of Litias, the soul of Litias, the feet of Litias, the body of Litias, and the head of Litias. I put under a spell to Hermes Katochos Nicias, the hands of that member of the Areopagus Council, and the feet, the tongue, and the body of Nicias. I put under a spell to Hermes Katochos Demetrius, and the body, the work, the hands, the feet, and the soul of Demetrius the pot-mender. I put under a spell to Hermes Katochos Epicharinus. I put under a spell to Hermes Katochos Demades the pot-mender, and his body and work and soul. I put under a spell [. . . .]. I put under a spell to Hermes Katochos Daphnis. I put under a spell to Hermes Katochos Philonides. I put under a spell, I put under a spell to Hermes Katochos Simale and Piste.
>
> I put under a spell to Persephone and Hades Litias, the feet, the hands, the soul, and the body of Litias, the tongue of Litias, the plans of Litias, and whatever he labors at.
>
> (Peek, Kerameikos, vol. 3, no. 9)

Let Pherenicus be put under a spell to Hermes Chthonikos and Hecate Chthonia. And I put under a spell to Hermes Chthonikos and Hecate Chthonia Galene,[9] who associates with Pherenicus. And just as this lead is cold and is held in no esteem, so may Pherenicus and his things be cold and held in no esteem, and so may be the things which Pherenicus' collaborators say and plot concerning me.

> Let Thersilochus, Oenophilus, Philotius, and any
> other legal supporter of Pherenicus be put under a spell
> to Hermes Chthonikos and Hecate Chthonia. And I put
> under a spell the soul and mind and tongue and plans of
> Pherenicus, and whatever he does and plots concerning
> me. Let all things be opposed to him[10] and to those who
> plot and act with him.
>
> (Wünsch, *Defixionum Tabellae*, no. 107)

Evidently the soul of the deceased was expected to hand over,
like a letter, to Hermes or Persephone the messages scratched
on these tablets.[11]

Some apparently believed that the souls of the dead resided
not in the underworld but in the *aither*, or sky:

> Here lies the body of Eurymachus,
> But the moist air above now holds his soul
> And his powerful intelligence.
>
> (Peek, *GV* no. 1755 = *IG* II^2 11466)

This epitaph and the one other similar to it from the fourth
century (Peek, *GV* no. 595 = *IG* II^2 13104/5) may derive from
the famous public epitaph of the Athenians who died in battle
at Potidaea in 432.[12] The belief that the soul resided in the sky,
although not widely attested in sources for popular religion,
was familiar enough to Athenians for Aristophanes to use it as
the basis of a humorous description of a journey in outer space
(*Pax* 827–841). There was also current, at least in philosophical
circles, the fear "that when the soul departs from the body it no
longer exists anywhere, but is destroyed on the very day on
which a man dies, as soon as it departs from the body" (Plato
Phd. 69E–70A).

The epitaphs give no description of the life of the soul in the
underworld or in the sky. In an earlier period it had been believed that a homicide victim left behind him "avenging spirits"
and that these spirits harassed the murderer, but this belief does
not appear current in the fourth century.[13] In matters besides
murder the orators could, as their argument required, either

claim or deny that the dead had perception of the acts of the living. It is occasionally said, although very tentatively, that the dead were watching the outcome of a trial.[14] Aeschines (1.14), on the other hand, denies, quite confidently and matter-of-factly, that the dead have perception even of their own funerals. I suspect that claims that the dead might have perception of life in the upper world arose from the orators' appeal to the sentimentality rather than to the religious beliefs of their audiences.

Public orations for the state funerals of those who had died in war provided the occasion for outpourings of emotional and patriotic sentiments, and in our sources it is only in such orations that we have portrayals of life in the underworld. Even these portrayals are brief and bare, however, with Hyperides (6.35), for example, claiming that Leosthenes, the hero of the unsuccessful Athenian revolt against Macedonia in 323, "might" see the great Homeric heroes welcoming him in the underworld. Demosthenes (60.34) says that the war dead "might" dwell with the good men of the past on the "Islands of the Blessed."[15] It would appear that these orators, in their attempts to eulogize the war dead, reached beyond popular religious conceptions and introduced literary and mythological themes. The pale, almost non-existence in the afterlife was not a sufficient reward for these new national heroes, and for them the orators had to enhance the afterlife with features from literature and mythology.[16]

In their funeral orations Hyperides and Demosthenes each suggest that the war dead might be rewarded in the afterlife for the virtue they demonstrated in this life.[17] Hyperides (6.43) speaks directly of these rewards:

> If death is like nonexistence, these men are freed from diseases and suffering and from the other things which beset the life of a human being. But if men have perception in the house of Hades and if they are cared for by the daimonic [element], as we suspect they are, then it is

reasonable to assume that those who defended the
abused honors of the gods find the greatest care from the
daimonic [element].

In a very private and tender manner Hippostrate, a young girl,
expresses much the same thought in the epitaph for her nurse
Melitta:

> Melitta, daughter of Apollodorus.
> Here lies beneath the earth Hippostrate's good nurse.
> And how Hippostrate now longs for you!
> I loved you so, dear nurse,
> And now, for all my life,
> I'll honor you, though you lie below.
> If the good receive a prize in the underworld,
> You now, I know, enjoy first place
>   with Pluto and Persephone.[18]
>   (Peek, *GV* no. 747 = *IG* II² 7873)

A similar reward is suggested in another epitaph:

> Your virtue, Nicoptoleme, endures
> Undying in your husband's memory.
> If piety finds favor with Persephone,[19]
> Fortune, through death, grants this reward to you.
>   (Peek, *GV* no. 1491 = *IG* II² 6551)

Each of these expressions of hope for rewards in the afterlife is
limited by a condition. For Hippostrate the uncertainty is "if
the good receive a prize in the underworld"; for Hyperides, "if
men have perception in the house of Hades and if they are
cared for by the daimonic [element]"; and for the author of the
epitaph, "if piety finds favor with Persephone." The uncertainty
in each instance focuses on a different area, but it is clear that
even the most positive expressions of hopes for rewards in the
afterlife were riddled with doubt. Against these few instances
in which hopes for rewards were expressed we must balance the
hundreds of epitaphs in which the individual's virtues were
listed but there is no indication of hope for rewards in the after-

life. One must, I think, conclude from these epitaphs that the expectation of rewards for virtue in the afterlife was not only very uncertain, but also very uncommon. This conclusion is admittedly drawn *ex silentio*, but where might one find such expectations expressed if not on the epitaphs which record the virtues? One must conclude, I think, that most Athenians did *not* expect to be rewarded in the afterlife for the virtues, including piety, which they demonstrated in this life.

Nor did they, as a general rule, expect punishment in the afterlife for their vices and sins. In our sources it is only the aged Cephalus who, in a Platonic dialogue (*Rep.* 1.330D–331B), begins to think seriously about the possible punishments after death:

> When the thought of his own death approaches a man, he feels fear and concern about things about which he did not before. The stories that are told about the things in Hades, that the man who acted unjustly in this world must pay the penalty there, are laughed at until this time, but then the fear that they may be true racks his soul. And either because of the weakness of old age or because he is now closer to Hades, he himself sees these things more clearly and is filled with suspicion and terror. Then a man does his accounts and examines whether he has committed any injustice against anyone. The man who discovers unjust acts in his life wakes up from sleep frequently like children and is terrified and lives with a bad hope for the future. But the man who knows of no unjust acts which he has committed always has a hope that is sweet and, as Pindar says, a good "nurse of his old age." For in a charming way Pindar said this, Socrates, that if a man lives his life in a just and holy manner,
>
> > Sweet hope, which guides man's roving thought,
> > A nurse of his old age,
> > Attends and nourishes his heart.
>
> It is remarkable how well Pindar puts this. In this respect I consider the possession of wealth most valuable, not for

every man, but for the man who is good and decent. For the possession of wealth contributes much to not deceiving and cheating anyone involuntarily and to going to the afterlife not owing sacrifices to a god or money to a man.

Cephalus uses his wealth to square his accounts with men and gods[20] and thereby hedges his bet in case the stories about Hades put forward by the Orphics and others might be true.[21]

In our sources, apart from Cephalus, we find no statement of the expectation of punishment in the afterlife. It is most revealing, I think, that we do not find it in those cases where we should most expect it, that is, when speakers are attacking villainous, perjured, and impious men. In all such cases the descriptions of the expected sufferings of the malefactor stop with his death. Punishment after death is not introduced for murderers, perjurors, or perpetrators of other impious acts. The punishment might fall upon the malefactor's children,[22] but it does not seem to have pursued the criminal himself after his death. It is also noteworthy that in the curses accompanying oaths individuals put under a curse only elements of this life such as their own lives, property, and families.[23] One did *not* threaten for oneself punishments in the afterlife. The conclusion must be that Athenians in the fourth century generally did not foresee such punishments for misdeeds in this life. This conclusion, which also must be based on an argument *ex silentio*, is supported by Isocrates' comparison of immortal cities to mortal men (8.120): "Cities much more than individuals ought to practise virtues and to avoid evil actions. A man who is impious and wicked might happen to die before he pays the penalty for his misdeeds, but because cities are immortal they face punishment both from men and from the gods."

Cephalus wishes to have, in the face of death, "sweet hope," and Isocrates (4.28) tells us that it is precisely "sweeter hopes concerning the end of life and all eternity" which initiates in the Eleusinian Mysteries received. Aristophanes (*Ra.* 154–158) portrays the initiates enjoying eternal light, music, and dancing in the afterlife. The object of Cephalus' and Isocrates' "sweet hopes" may have been something of this type, but there is no indication in the epitaphs or in the other sources for popular religion that individuals expected or hoped for this type of life after death. The secrecy surrounding the Eleusinian Mysteries may have inhibited public expression of these hopes, and the relative lack of evidence blocks our understanding of what initiation meant for an individual's afterlife. But, in any case, the silence in our sources may belie the great importance usually attributed to the Mysteries for ordinary Athenians. All we can say is that, if there was a large group of Athenians who expected a blessed afterlife because they were initiated into the Mysteries, they have very successfully concealed from us their existence.

In summary, then, the average Athenian foresaw in the afterlife, if anything, his soul residing in the underworld, in the "chamber" of Persephone. Various mythological, literary, and philosophical descriptions of the underworld were current and familiar, but none seems to have won general acceptance. And with the possible exception of initiates in the Eleusinian Mysteries, the average Athenian expected neither rewards nor punishments in the afterlife for his deeds in this life. Clearly what mattered to the average Athenian was this life, and in the fourth century he took little interest in the bleak and uncertain prospect of the afterlife.

ELEVEN

Some Social Aspects of
Popular Religion

The social, political, and religious life of the Athenian citizen in this period was largely structured by his membership in his polis, tribe, deme, phratry, genos, and family.[1] Religion was a significant part of the identity and function of these and most other Athenian social and political groups.[2] Each of these groups had a separate center for its religious activity. In Athens the religious center for the polis was, generally speaking, the Acropolis;[3] for the boule, the altars of Zeus Boulaios and Athena Boulaia in the bouleuterion; for the tribes, the sanctuaries of the heroes after whom they were named; for the demes, sacred areas such as the Pagus in Erchia[4] or the sanctuary of the goddess Hebe in Aexone (*IG* II[2] 1199); for the gene and phratries, the local cult centers and meeting places like that of the Demotionidae, Deceleieis, and Salaminioi;[5] and for the families, the homes. The religious activities of a group might occur in different places. A family, for example, might perform traditional rites for the dead at family tombs and also maintain the cults of Zeus Ktesios and Zeus Herkeios in the home.[6] But for the most part there was one physical center of a group's religious activity, and that religious center was at or near the place where the group regularly met.

A deity such as Zeus Boulaios or Zeus Phratrios owed his existence and nature to the group and was inextricably associated with it. Such a deity functioned and was worshiped only within the framework of the group with which he was identified. The polis, since it incorporated all smaller units, might establish one state sanctuary of, for example, Zeus Phratrios or Zeus Ktesios,[7] but this was secondary and, I suspect, largely symbolic. The true cult and function of such deities lay within the smaller individual groups.

In accordance with the general Athenian respect for the priority of the gods, many or perhaps all of these social and political groups began their meetings with purifications, sacrifices, and prayers.[8] Communal prayers, libations, and sacrifices with their accompanying banquets are well attested for the members of the boule, prytany, deme, phratry, genos, and family, and even of the official boards of generals and such officials.[9] Within each group certain individuals, such as the demarch ("deme-chief") for the deme ([Dem.] 43.57–58; Erchia calendar; *IG* II[2] 1177), the phratriarch ("phratry-chief") or the priest of Zeus Phratrios for the phratry (*IG* II[2] 1237), and the father for the family (Isaeus 8.15–16), had the responsibility for performing the religious ritual of the group.[10] In the Athenian polis as a whole the responsibility for religious ritual had become fragmented to a certain extent, but the archon with the title *basileus* ("king") maintained authority over several of the older cults (Arist. *Ath. Pol.* 57.1–2; [Dem.] 59.74–77; Plato *Plt.* 290E).

The group was able to introduce new members and to expel former ones. The introduction of new members was regularly attended by religious ritual of some type. Children were admitted into the family by the ritual of the Amphidromia, in which the parents of the five-day-old infant ran around the family hearth carrying the baby.[11] Friends and relatives sent presents and the women who had participated in the delivery were purified. On the tenth day after birth the parents named the child and invited relatives and close friends to a banquet which followed the sacrifices.[12] New slaves and in-laws were admitted into the family in a shower of "dates, small cakes, sweetmeats, dried figs, and nuts."[13] The elaborate rituals of the Apaturia es-

tablished full membership in the phratry. The phratries cele-
brated this three-day festival individually in the month Pyanop-
sion with feasting and sacrificing. On the final day fathers
presented their sons to the phratry and swore oaths concerning
their eligibility for membership. The young men made sacrificial offerings, and the members voted on membership by taking their ballots from the altar of Zeus Phratrios. If the young
man was accepted, he became a member of the phratry. If re-
jected, he could appeal the vote through the court system.[14]
Wives were introduced into the phratry by the Gamelia, which
was a sacrifice, banquet, or cash donation given to members of
the phratry by the husband.[15] Rituals like those of the Apaturia
may have been a part of the introduction into the genos.[16] In
this period membership in the phratry was tantamount to
membership in the deme, and we find only oaths sworn by individuals as religious elements in the admission to the deme
and to certain other political and social groups of the state as a
whole such as the boule and the archonships.[17] It was the
"ephebic" oath which solemnized a young man's entrance into
full citizenship in the state.[18] In this oath he swore to maintain
or enlarge and better the fatherland as a whole, to hold in
honor the ancestral sanctuaries, to obey the officials and laws of
the state, and to be a courageous soldier. The young man stood
in full armor and swore this oath in the sanctuary of the goddess Aglaurus on the north slope of the Acropolis.

The group was a closed organization which could, however,
choose to extend participation in certain areas to nonmembers.[19] The genos of the Eumolpidae, for example, extended to
Tlepolemus, because of his zealousness concerning sacred matters and the genos, the right of receiving a portion of meat like
that of the Eumolpidae from the sacrifices at the Mysteries of
Eleusis and Agrae (*IG* II[2] 1231). The demesmen of Lamptrae
extended to Philocedes of the deme Acharnae (*IG* II[2] 1204) a
similar privilege. The group might, of course, reserve some of
its religious practices only for members while granting the right
to some nonmembers to participate in others. The demesmen
of Piraeus did this in the limited rights they granted to Cal-

lidamas (*IG* II² 1187). Personal preferences in such matters might vary considerably, and Ciron, for example, limited his familial sacrifices to Zeus Ktesios to freeborn, legitimate members of his family (Isaeus 8.15–16). Philius, on the other hand, invited to his sacrifice to the same god not his wife and children but a concubine and a friend (Antiphon 1.16–20). The inclusion of a nonmember into the group is always treated as a mark of special friendship, gratitude, and honor, and since our sources treat such inclusion as a special situation, it is apparent that these groups were generally concerned to limit their religious as well as their other activities to their own members. This was particularly important in religious matters because proper performance of religious ritual required a knowledge of the religious traditions of the group. For this reason in Athens "naturalized" citizens were not allowed to hold priesthoods or other state offices which tended state cults:

> The law expressly forbids those whom the Athenian people have made citizens to become one of the nine archons or to hold any priesthood. But the people have granted to the descendants of these a share in all these things, and have added as a condition, "if the descendants are born from a woman who is a citizen and is legally married."
>
> ([Dem.] 59.92)

The legitimate children of naturalized citizens presumably would come to know Athenian traditions, and therefore they were allowed, like born Athenians, to hold these offices after they attained the required age.

These groups which had religious as well as political or social functions could expel members for religious reasons. A law attributed to the early sixth-century lawgiver Solon placed strict limitations on the communal religious activities of cowards:

> The lawgiver Solon excludes from the purified areas of the marketplace the man who has shirked military service [20] and the coward and the man who has abandoned

his military post, nor does he allow him to wear a garland or to be admitted to public sacrifices.

(Aeschines 3.176)

The murderer, as was discussed above,[21] was excluded by law
from purifications, libations, wine-bowls, sanctuaries, sacrifices, contests, the marketplace, and even the city itself. Solo-
nian laws also excluded adulteresses from the sanctuaries of
the city:

> A woman with whom an adulterer is caught is not per-
> mitted to enter any of the public sanctuaries.[22] The laws
> granted permission even to foreign women and slave
> women to enter the sanctuaries in order to see them and
> to make supplications. But the laws forbid the entering
> of public sanctuaries to a woman with whom an adul-
> terer is caught, and if they do enter and transgress the
> law, the law allows them to suffer without redress any
> punishment, except death, at the hands of anyone who
> wishes to inflict it, and the law has granted to any
> passerby the right to exact the punishment for these mat-
> ters. The law provides that she may in no way get redress
> when she has been maltreated in all other ways except
> death so that pollutions and impieties may not be in the
> sanctuaries. The law creates for the women fear sufficient
> to motivate temperate behavior, the avoidance of wrong-
> doing, and a law-abiding desire to stay at home, because
> it teaches them that if a woman commits any such wrong
> she will at the same time be thrown out from her hus-
> band's house and from the sanctuaries of the city. And
> you shall know that these things are so when you have
> heard the law itself read. Read it for me.

LAW OF ADULTERY

> "When a husband catches the adulterer, let it not be per-
> mitted for the husband to live with his wife. And if he
> does live with her, let him lose his citizen-rights. And let
> the woman with whom an adulterer is caught not be per-

mitted to enter into the public sanctuaries. But if she
does enter, let her suffer whatever she may suffer, except
death, without redress."[23]

([Dem.] 59.85–87)

Murderers and adulteresses may originally have been excluded from the sanctuaries because they were thought to be
polluted, and as such they not only generally caused ill-fortune
but they specifically endangered the success of religious rituals.[24] Our sources, however, do not stress the fact of pollution
and its effects, but rather emphasize in these cases the importance of law.[25] The laws in these matters were attributed to
Draco and Solon, in whose time belief in pollution may have
been considerably stronger than it was in the fourth century. It
is to these laws, and not to the evils of pollution itself, that our
sources usually turn when they describe cowards, murderers,
and adulteresses. Several sources also view the exclusion of such
persons from religious activities as an effective social deterrent
for others who might contemplate committing similar acts.[26]

Much of what has been said concerning the polis, tribe,
deme, phratry, genos, and family may be applied also to similar, sometimes less formal social and political groups. The
members of a prytany, for example, and the board of generals
each performed religious ritual as a group (Dem. 19.190). For
all the groups inclusion of a nonmember was a mark of friendship and honor; the exclusion of a member was a sign of rejec-
tion and disgrace. Even such a loose and *ad hoc* group as pris-
oners in a jail could exclude a man, for unspeakable acts, from
its meals and its sacrifices (Dinarchus 2.9).[27]

It is interesting to note that although most of a citizen's religious activities took place within a group, beliefs and practices
which are generally labeled superstitious are mostly asocial.
The "superstitious man" of Theophrastus (*Char.* 16) nearly always acts alone. The vagabond priests whom Plato describes
(*Rep.* 2.364B–C) functioned independently, outside the traditional social groups of Athenian society:

Soothsayers and vagabond priests go to the doors of the wealthy, and as if they possessed a power provided to them from the gods because of their sacrifices and incantations, they persuade the wealthy man that they can remedy with pleasures and religious celebrations any injustice which the wealthy man himself or his ancestors may have committed. And if the wealthy man wishes to harm some enemy, they say that at little cost they will harm a just man as well as an unjust man with some invocations and spells.[28] They do this, as they say, by persuading the gods to serve them.

Soothsayers such as Thrasyllus (Isoc. 19.5–7) and Sthorys, being itinerants, necessarily functioned outside established social and political groups.[29] A successful soothsayer like Sthorys might be awarded Athenian citizenship or like Thrasyllus might retire to his homeland after he had acquired a fortune, but professionally they dealt mostly with individuals on an *ad hoc* basis, apart from the established cults and social groups of the community in which they practised.

There were times in their lives when all individuals, and not just the superstitious, privately performed sacrifices and directed prayers to the gods. In times of personal need for health, safety, money, and such things individuals personally made sacrifices, uttered prayers, and erected dedications.[30] But it would appear from our sources that religious activities which were intended simply to maintain the goodwill of the gods, those activities which were performed on a regular basis throughout one's life, were all social activities which the individual performed as a member of a group. On such occasions one gathered around himself, if the structure of the group permitted it, his close family and friends.[31] It is the mark of the "shameless man" intentionally to exclude from such activities his family and friends. Theophrastus' (*Char.* 9.2) "shameless man, when he has performed a sacrifice to the gods, salts and stores away the meat and then goes to dine at another's house." We can see here, without denying the solemnity of the religious ritual, an association of "sacrificing" and "banqueting," an association found elsewhere.[32] Most sacrifices afforded the participants the rare opportunity for a splendid dinner with abundant meat, and to deny one's relatives and friends this pleasure may not have been impious but it was certainly gauche.

Piety and Impiety

Piety and impiety are best treated together because what the Athenians say of impiety most often sheds some light on their concept of piety, and vice versa.[1] Occasionally we have both the positive and negative aspects defined, with, for example, the maintenance of an oath described as "pious" but the violation of an oath described as "impious." Descriptions of impiety are, however, more frequent than those of piety, and therefore most often we have only the one term specified, with, for example, the robbing of a sanctuary designated "impious." In this case, presumably, the opposite or the nonperformance of the deed was considered either "pious" or neutral. What follows is a catalogue of those acts which the sources designate as pious or impious, and this catalogue will serve to outline roughly those aspects of life in which the Athenians believed piety was involved. This catalogue is divided, somewhat schematically, according to the primary element which the Athenians thought determined the piety or impiety of an act. These determinants appear to be the legal system, tradition, and a general, informal consensus of opinion somewhat distinct from the other two. These divisions are not, of course, exclusive, and each determinant is a factor to some extent in most matters concerning piety and impiety, but the sources do seem to agree in stressing the primacy of one of these determinants in specific cases.

On various occasions individuals were brought to trial through the legal system on charges of impiety.[2] Permission to bring individuals to trial on such charges was obtained from the basileus, who had inherited some of the religious powers and duties of the old kings.[3] The specific charges attested for these trials in the late fifth and fourth centuries include: introducing a new god; participating in religious revelry in a shameless manner; assembling illegal religious groups of men and women; revealing, vulgarizing, and belittling the Eleusinian Mysteries; and mutilating the statues of Hermes.[4] The prosecutors in these cases may well have been motivated by personal enmities or political allegiances, but this does not invalidate the conclusion that acts of this type were considered impious and were thought to be the legitimate concern of Athenian law courts.[5]

To the extent that religious beliefs and acts can be separated, the trials for impiety in this period centered on acts rather than on beliefs.[6] Even the charges of impiety brought against Socrates in 399, however vague they may have been and however many other factors were involved,[7] were viewed by at least some of Socrates' contemporaries in terms of impious acts. The impiety charge against him was twofold, that "he does not recognize gods whom the city recognizes but is introducing other new daimonic [powers]."[8] There were a number of laws concerning such matters. A law of Draco (Porphyry *Abst.* 4.22) reportedly bade the Athenians "as a group to honor the gods and local heroes in accordance with the ancestral practices, and in private as best they can, with pious language and with first-fruit offerings of produce and with annual offerings of cakes." A decree proposed by Diopeithes and enacted by the ecclesia ca. 433 bade that those who "did not respect the divine things" be brought to trial for impiety (Plut. *Per.* 32.2). "To respect the gods" (or "divine things") could mean, at different times and to different people, either "to observe proper cult practices concerning the gods" or "to believe that the gods exist."[9] And, finally, Josephus (*Ap.* 2.267) reports an Athenian law, used against the priestess Ninus, which forbade the importation of a "foreign god." In practical terms the establishment of a foreign cult in Athens required the ecclesia's approval in order to purchase land for a cult center. The Egyptian devotees of Isis and the Cyprian ones of Aphrodite Ourania, for example, had to secure this approval from the ecclesia (*IG* II² 337) before they built their sanctuaries.

The arguments of Socrates' defenders, Plato and Xenophon, suggest that the charges against him were taken by some of his contemporaries to mean that he failed to observe proper cult practices and that he, like the courtesan Phryne, introduced the cult of a new deity.[10] Plato and Xenophon stressed throughout their writings that Socrates had participated in and urged the observance of traditional cults.[11] In regard to the introduction of "new daimonic [powers]," Plato was led to suggest that the deity whom Socrates allegedly introduced was his "daimonion," his personal divinatory voice (*Ap.* 31C–D, *Euthyphr.* 3B). Xenophon in his defenses of Socrates (*Mem.* 1.1.2–3, *Ap.* 24) made a particular effort to demonstrate that Socrates did not treat this daimonion as a cult figure. The details of the charges of impiety were apparently never spelled out, even in the course of the trial, and much uncertainty still surrounds them. But in any case the defenses of Plato and Xenophon reveal that to some of Socrates' contemporaries the issue was acts rather than beliefs and teachings.

Apart from trials specifically for impiety there were also trials for acts of which impiety was an important, though not primary, factor. Foremost among these was murder. In the fourth century the pollution of the murderer was regularly noted, and because of this pollution the murderer was excluded "from the water of purification, from libations, from the wine-bowls, from the sanctuaries," from "sacrifices and contests," and from the marketplace and the city itself.[12] Those who hindered the proper conviction and punishment of the murderer could share in the impiety as well as in the pollution of the murderer himself.[13] The proper punishment of murderers was thought "to increase the number of those who practise piety" (Antiphon 2.3.9–11). Antiphon (4.1.2–4) considered the act of murder impious because it destroyed a life which "the god" valued and nurtured, and Lysias once claims (13.3) that if the Athenians duly exacted vengeance from a murderer it would be better for them "on the part of both gods and men." Antiphon's statement that "the god" was angry at the destruction of a life he valued has the flavor of rationalizing. The introduction of the Olympian gods into the realms of murder, although it is very rare in this period, may be a reflection of weakening belief in the "avenging spirits" and pollution which once dominated the religious aspects of murder.[14]

Traitors, according to Lycurgus (*Leoc.* 129), commit impiety because they "deprive the gods of their ancestral and traditional cults." Lycurgus implicitly contrasted his own piety to the impiety of the traitorous Leocrates when he opened his speech against Leocrates (1–2) with this prayer:

> I pray to Athena and to the other gods and heroes who are established throughout this city and land to make me on this day a worthy prosecutor of the crimes of Leocrates if I have impeached him justly and if I bring to trial a man who has betrayed their temples, statues, sacred precincts, their honors established in the laws, and the sacrifices handed down by our ancestors.

All Athenian male citizens had sworn the ephebic oath, which included provisions to maintain or enlarge and better the fatherland, to hold in honor the ancestral sanctuaries, to obey the officials and laws, and not to desert comrades-in-arms on the battlefield.[15] A traitor who had sworn this oath was therefore guilty not only of the impiety of treason but also of the impiety of perjury (Lycurgus *Leoc.* 76). The gods were thought to demonstrate their hostility to traitors by refusing them help (*Leoc.* 129) and by aiding in their prosecution.[16] And the law, it appears, put traitors and temple-robbers on a par:

> The law applies to the temple-robbers and traitors and states that if anyone betrays the city or steals from the sanctuaries, if he has been tried and convicted in court, he is not to be buried in Attica and his property is to be confiscated.
>
> (Xen. *Hell.* 1.7.22)

The Athenians went so far as to exhume and remove from their country the bones of a traitor:

> On the motion of Critias the people voted to bring to trial the corpse on the charge of treason, and if it appeared that Phrynichus had been buried in the country when he was in fact a traitor, to exhume his bones and to take them outside of the boundaries of Attica so that not even the bones of a man who betrays his land and city might lie in their country.
>
> (Lycurgus *Leoc.* 113)

Those who had died in service to their country were, of course, the antithesis to those who had committed treason. Their actions, though not generally designated "pious," deserved "honors equal to those of the gods."[17] In prehistoric times this might mean that they became heroes of the type after whom the ten tribes were eventually named (Dem. 60.27–31), but in contemporary times it meant that they received the annual funeral games directed by an archon.[18] In public eulogies the orators foresaw for them, probably overenthusiastically, a heroes' reception in the afterlife.[19]

There were other impious acts which could entail prosecution in the courts; these included robbing sanctuaries and chopping down the sacred olive trees.[20] The severity of the punishment in both cases—death—indicates the religious aspects of these crimes. Wood was a precious commodity in Attica, and even the unauthorized gathering of it from sanctuaries could result in, if not a charge of impiety, at least corporal punishments for slaves and fines for freemen.[21] The charge of unauthorized collection of wood from a sanctuary, like charges of impiety, was lodged with the basileus.

Tradition was a dominant factor in the maintenance of religious beliefs and practices in all aspects of ancient religion. It determined the rituals of major religious festivals with much the same force as it determined the petty precautions of Theophrastus' superstitious man, and it contributed as much to beliefs concerning divination as it did to those concerning the afterlife. Here, however, I wish to treat tradition only to the extent that the Athenians themselves stressed its importance in particular areas of religious belief and practice.

Athenians of the fourth century invoked the importance of tradition in matters of cult, especially in matters of sacrifice, and also in the rites of the dead and of the family in general. "Ancestral practices" (τὰ πάτρια), "customary practices" (τὰ εἰθότα), and "traditional rites" (τὰ νομιζόμενα) were the phrases commonly used of numerous sacrifices and rituals.[22] These ranged from elaborate sacrifices offered by the state in public festivals to the private offerings of families.

The Athenian view of "ancestral sacrifices" is well summarized by Isocrates in the *Areopagiticus*, a political pamphlet in which he promotes some conservative social and political reforms (7.29–30):

> First of all in matters concerning the gods—for it is right to begin from there—our ancestors did not perform the services and celebrate the rites in an irregular and disorganized fashion. Nor did they send in procession three hundred cattle whenever it struck their fancy, nor did they leave aside the ancestral sacrifices on chance occasions. Nor did they celebrate with great grandeur the new festivals in which a feast was included, nor in the most sacred of sacrifices did they make their offerings through [contractors and] contracts. They guarded against the elimination of any of the ancestral sacrifices and against the addition of any sacrifices outside the traditional ones. For they thought that piety consisted not in great expenditures, but rather in not changing any of those things which their ancestors had handed down to them. And furthermore, help from the gods occurred for them not in fits and starts and not confusedly, but at the proper time both for the working of the land and for the harvest of the produce.

It was impious not to make the traditional sacrifices as well as to make them in the wrong manner.[23] The introduction of new sacrifices was suspect and might even be impious if it led to

abandonment or change of the traditional ones.[24] Oracles
(Dem. 21.51–53; [Dem.] 43.66) regularly ordered the performance of these traditional sacrifices. The law ([Dem.] 59.92)
which denied to naturalized citizens the right to hold an ar-
chonship or a priesthood was intended to ensure that "the sacrifices on behalf of the city are made piously." The children of
such naturalized citizens would have become familiar with the
Athenian religious traditions, and when they attained the required age they were allowed to hold such offices.

Tradition was also invoked for the rituals associated with the
dead. The rites for the dead were simply called "the traditional
rites."[25] This term designated individually or as a group the funeral rites and later rituals for the dead such as the banquets on
the third (*trita*), ninth (*enata*), and thirtieth (*triakas*) days after
burial and the later annual presentation of offerings and libations at the tomb.[26] "The concern of the gods," according to
Lycurgus (*Leoc.* 94), "watches over all human actions, and especially over those involving parents and the dead." Leocrates,
in depriving his ancestors of their traditional rites by his flight
from his endangered homeland, was committing an act of impiety (*Leoc.* 97). An individual such as Macartatus ([Dem.]
43.65) or Chariades (Isaeus 4.19) could be termed "unholy" if
he claimed the right to inherit a dead man's property when he
had not performed the traditional rites for him.

When the Pythia, Apollo's spokeswoman in Delphi, was
asked what constituted pious behavior concerning sacrifices or
the cult of ancestors, she responded that men "would be acting
piously if they acted in accordance with the law of the city"
(Xen. *Mem.* 1.3.1). By "the law of the city" we should assume, I
think, law (νόμος) in its broadest range to include traditions as
well as formal statutes. Laws in the strict sense did operate in
this area. For example, one law bade a maltreated son to bury
his father and "to perform the other traditional rites" (Aeschines 1.13–14). But although various aspects of the burial and cult
of the dead may have been the subject of legislation (e.g.,
[Dem.] 43.57–58), the Athenians by the very name they gave to
these rites stressed the primacy of tradition.

In the family cult of such domestic deities as Zeus Ktesios,

Zeus Herkeios, and Apollo Agyieus,[27] the primary determinant
of piety was tradition, and Lycurgus (*Leoc.* 25) attacks Leocrates for removing from Athens and erecting in the foreign en-
vironment of Megara his "ancestral holy objects." One element
of the exceptional piety of Clearchus of Methydrion (Porphyry
Abst. 2.16) was that "on the first day of each month he garlanded and polished Hermes and Hecate and the rest of the sacred things which his ancestors had passed down to him."[28]

The Athenians stressed tradition in matters concerning cult,
in sacrifices, rituals, and tendance of the dead, and in the maintenance of family religious practices. Piety, in these areas, consisted "in not changing any of those things which their ancestors had handed down to them."[29]

Into the third category of acts of piety and impiety fall those
acts for which the Athenians stressed neither law nor tradition,
but for which they acknowledged a consensus of opinion. Law
and tradition surely influenced Athenian thought also in these
matters, but the Athenians themselves did not stress their
importance.

The maintenance of oaths was a key element of piety. We
have already examined its relationship to the more general concept of piety, the Athenians' establishment of religious sanctions for basically profane acts through promissory oaths, and
the gods' punishment of perjury.[30] These need be reviewed
only briefly here. Xenophon (*Ages.* 3.1–5) apparently believed
that a demonstration of Agesilaus' maintenance of his oaths
was a sufficient proof of Agesilaus' piety in general. Other
sources, although not going this far, always give the maintenance of oaths particular emphasis in discussions of piety. The
gods punished the perjuror, usually by effecting the curse at-
tached to the oath, and the perjuror could not expect to escape
divine punishment by fleeing to "any dark spot." Should the
perjuror himself somehow escape punishment, his children
might pay for his impiety. The very frequent use of oaths in all
aspects of Athenian life[31] suggests that here especially the individual Athenian most often faced squarely a choice between

pious and impious action. It was in this area that an individual might frequently encounter conflicts between financial or social gain and personal piety. And since there were no trials or legal punishments for perjury itself, except as false testimony in court,[32] the choice between financial or social gain on the one hand and personal or socially recognized piety on the other might be particularly stark. It may be just for this reason that our sources treat the maintenance of oaths as the key, or at least as the most prominent, element of personal piety.

Respect of the rights of asylum, like the maintenance of oaths, was the mark of a pious man. Xenophon (*Ages.* 11.1–2) cites it as an example of piety in his encomium on Agesilaus, and in the *Hellenica* (2.3.51–55) Critias' seizure of Theramenes from the altar in the bouleuterion in 403 revealed the impious character of him and of the rest of the Thirty Tyrants. Similarly Aeschines (3.223–224) charged Demosthenes with an impious act for having tortured and put to death the pro-Macedonian Anaxinus of Oreus, with whom he had established a guest/host relationship. In Aeschines' view, at least, this relationship, which had religious foundations, outweighed even the welfare of the city. An adulteress was also considered impious and polluted ([Dem.] 59.85–87). She was excluded from the public sanctuaries, partially so that she might not morally corrupt other women (Aeschines 1.183) but partially because she, like a murderer, was polluted in religious terms ([Dem.] 59.85–87).

The piety of providing the "traditional rites" for one's dead parents has already been discussed, but Lycurgus in particular stressed the piety of caring well for one's parents while they were alive. "It is," he claimed (*Leoc.* 94), "the greatest impiety not to spend our lives benefiting those from whom we have received the beginning of life and those from whom we have ourselves received very many good things." And when Lycurgus charged against Leocrates (*Leoc.* 97) that "he deprived the gods of their ancestral honors, he abandoned his parents to the enemy, and he did not allow the dead to receive their traditional rites," he included the maltreatment of living parents with two other impious acts. And, finally, in his story of the eruption of

Mount Etna (*Leoc.* 95–96) Lycurgus illustrated the piety of devotion to one's parents even at the risk of one's own personal safety:

> [There is a story] which, even if it is rather mythical, will still be appropriate for all you younger men to hear. It is said that on Sicily a stream of lava arose from Etna. They say that this lava flowed over the rest of the land and was approaching one of the cities situated there. The other people sought their own safety and rushed off in flight, but one young man, when he saw that his father was too old to flee and was being overtaken by the lava, lifted him up and carried him. And because of the extra burden, I suppose, the young man himself was also caught in the lava. But from this event you ought to see that the divine is well-intentioned towards good men, because, as the story goes, that place was engulfed by lava and only this father and son survived. From them the place still even now is called "The place of the Pious." Those who tried to quicken their retreat by abandoning their parents all perished.

That Lycurgus' outlook in these matters was not idiosyncratic is suggested by the charge made against Philon (Lysias 31.20–21) that he had behaved so sinfully towards his mother when she was alive and after her death that he ought not to be admitted as a member to the boule. The Athenians went so far in these matters as to ask the archon-designate, in the examination required before he could assume office, "if he treats his parents well" (Arist. *Ath. Pol.* 55.1–3).

In order to win the favor of their audiences the Athenians commonly listed the money or services which they had provided for public religious purposes. A defendant charged with bribery and illegally holding state property provided his jury with an unusually detailed and lavish description of his contributions (Lysias 21.1–2):

> A sufficient demonstration has been given to you, men of the jury, concerning the charges. But I ask you to listen

also concerning the other things, so that you may know
what kind of a person I am when you vote on my case.
When Theopompus was archon [411/10] I passed the
scrutiny for citizenship and when appointed a choregus
for the tragic poets I spent 3,000 drachmas. And two
months later at the Thargelia I spent 2,000 drachmas for
my victory with the men's chorus. And when Glaucippus
was archon [410/9] I spent 800 drachmas for Pyrrhic
dancers in the Great Panathenaia. And, in addition, in
the same year, as choregus for the men in the Dionysia,
I won a victory, and together with the dedication of the
tripod I spent 5,000 drachmas. When Diocles was archon
[409/8] I spent 300 drachmas for a circular chorus in the
Small Panathenaia.[33]

Citizens were often honored for these contributions by the
group, usually the genos, tribe, or deme, which benefited.[34]
Public benefactors clearly felt little hesitation in publicizing
their services, [35] but it is noteworthy that they usually were
praised or praised themselves not for their piety, but for their
generosity. In our sources such generosity is associated with
piety only when the individuals involved performed some ritual acts in addition to giving donations.[36] The praise for piety
in these cases probably concerns the proper performance of
cult acts rather than the financial contribution itself.

There are traces of some criticism or at least skepticism concerning these lavish donations for public services. Lycurgus
(*Leoc.* 139), in speaking against a defendant who will no doubt
list his contributions, treats them largely as self-glorifying dem-
onstrations of wealth and, as such, inferior to contributions for
the maintenance of triremes and the building of city walls. A
story told by Theopompus, a Chian historian who resided in
Athens in the fourth century, reflects a more general skepticism
about the "pious" character of extravagant expenditures for religious purposes.[37]

Theopompus says that a Magnesian man came to Delphi
from Asia. He was very rich and possessed many herd
animals. This man was accustomed to make many grand

sacrifices to the gods each year, in part because of his
ready supply of victims, but in part because of his piety
and his wish to please the gods. With such a disposition
towards the divine he came to Delphi, and after he had
paraded his hecatomb for the god and after he had honored Apollo in a grand way he went into the oracle to
consult the god. He thought that he of all men gave the
best service to the gods, and therefore he asked the
Pythia to tell him who honored the divine best and most
eagerly, and who made the sacrifices which were most
pleasing to the gods. He assumed that he would be given
the first prize. But the priestess replied that the man who
best of all men served the gods was Clearchus, a man
who dwelled in Methydrion of Arcadia.

The Magnesian was astonished, and he greatly desired
to see and meet the man and to learn how he performed
his sacrifices. He therefore quickly went to Methydrion
and at first felt scorn for the smallness and poorness of
the place. He thought that no individual there, not even
the whole city itself, could honor the gods better and
more grandly than he. But when he met Clearchus he
asked him to tell him how he honored the gods. Clearchus said that he performed religious rights and zealously
sacrificed at the proper times. On the first of each month
he garlanded and polished Hermes and Hecate and the
rest of the sacred things which his ancestors had passed
down to him. He said he honored them with incense and
barleycakes and round cakes. And every year he participated in the state sacrifices and he did not neglect any
festival. And in all these sacrifices he served the gods not
by killing cattle and by butchering victims, but by offering whatever happened to be at hand. He said he carefully distributed to the gods the first-fruits offerings from
all the surplus fruits and produce which he received from
the land. Some of these he presented as they were and
some he burned for the gods.

(Porphyry *Abst.* 2.16)

The superiority of scrupulous maintenance of traditional cult practices over lavish expenditures which is reflected in this story is explicitly stated by Isocrates (7.29–30): "Our ancestors thought that piety consisted not in great expenditures, but rather in not changing any of those things which their ancestors had handed down to them."

A late author, attempting to provide a catalogue of the Aristotelian virtues and vices, claimed that "the first elements of just behavior are those concerning the gods, the daimons, the fatherland and parents, and the dead. Of these piety consists." "Impiety," he said, "is error concerning the gods and daimons, or concerning the dead, or concerning parents and the fatherland."[38] These summary accounts, although quite late and introducing a later concept of daimons,[39] provide a reasonably accurate and comprehensive synopsis of those areas in which Athenians of the fourth century believed piety and impiety were involved.[40] Maintenance of oaths, respect for the rights of asylum and hospitality, observance of tradition and law in cult matters of sacrifice and tendance of the dead, loyalty to one's country, and proper care of one's living parents were all elements of the pious life.[41] The reward for pious behavior was "the goodwill" of the gods, a goodwill which might result in material success and favorable opportunities for the individual and for the state.[42] The rewards for piety were thought to be, almost exclusively, in this life, and there is only the occasional vague and uncertain suggestion of some reward for piety in the afterlife.[43]

The individual or state that violated oaths, maltreated hosts or those having asylum, violated traditional practices in sacrifice and tendance of the dead, or committed a number of other impious acts incurred the hostility of the gods.[44] The individual who betrayed his country or neglected his living parents incurred this same hostility. This divine antagonism could, presumably, affect the individual's welfare in all those areas of life in which the gods intervened. Specific types of punishment were associated with certain types of impious behavior, and an individual might be condemned to death by a law court or lose his right to be buried in Attica, or he might find the gods serving him up for legal punishments.[45] In a few exceptional cases the impious man suffered dire physical ailments. Cinesias and his friends had mocked certain religious traditions, and he himself had defecated on statues of Hecate. His notorious impiety had been criticized by the comic poets,[46] and the speaker in a fragment of an oration of Lysias describes the punishment which the gods imposed upon Cinesias:

> Each of the others perished as you would expect such men to, but the gods put Cinesias, who was known to very many people, into such a condition that his enemies preferred that he live rather than die. The gods made him an example for other men, so that they might see that the gods do not put off the punishment of those who are excessively insolent towards divine matters upon their children, but they destroy miserably the sinners themselves by afflicting them with greater and harsher misfortunes and diseases than other men suffer. All of us by nature share in death and disease, but to continue in such a bad state so long and to be unable every day to end one's life by death befalls only those who have committed such sins as Cinesias has.
>
> (fragment 73 [Thalheim])

Descriptions of such direct intervention by the gods to punish impiety are rare and are confined to the late fifth and early fourth centuries.[47] But we find throughout the period the belief that an impious individual might cause the destruction of his house and family.[48] Common also was the belief that those who did not punish impious malefactors when given the opportunity might share in their impiety and punishments.[49] But all punishments for impiety, like the rewards for piety, were limited to this life.

In general terms the Athenians believed that piety was a necessary, though not sufficient, cause of national and personal prosperity. The vast majority of Athenians would have agreed,

I think, both with Antiphon (6.5) when he claimed that "a man who acts impiously and transgresses against the gods would deprive himself of the very hopes which are the greatest good men have," and with Isocrates (15.281–282) when he exhorted the Greeks "to think that those who get more from the gods both now and in the future are those who are most pious and most diligent in their tendance of the gods."

The Consensus

My method in preparing this study was first to determine what were the reliable sources for popular religious beliefs and secondly to gather from these sources all the material of a religious character. The sources, selected on the basis of principles described in the Introduction, were primarily the orators, Xenophon, and the inscriptions from late fifth- and fourth-century Athens. No statement about religious matters from a reliable source was excluded because it was at variance with other sources or because it seemed to be isolated or idiosyncratic. Each source which has something new or different to say about religious belief has been noted in the discussions.

Despite the inclusion of virtually all the material from these sources, a remarkable homogeneity and consensus of religious beliefs emerges. This consensus is in marked contrast to the impression one has of Greek religion if one studies it using evidence from disparate cities and historical periods. There was clearly in Athens in this period an established and widely accepted body of religious beliefs. The orators could make casual reference to this corpus and could expect to find general acceptance for their statements.

The agreement among the sources is easily recognizable in the preceding discussions of various religious topics. The extent of this consensus can perhaps be best suggested by showing it in those places where one would least expect it, that is, in those pairs of speeches in which the speakers are arguing against one another. The speakers are at pains to demonstrate the falseness of their opponents' positions, and it is instructive to note how they handle religious points in these arguments.

The arguments in the *Tetralogies* of Antiphon provide one clear, though artificial example of this type.[1] Each *Tetralogy* is based on a hypothetical homicide trial and consists of two speeches for the prosecution and two for the defense. In all cases the prosecution and the defense accept the belief that the homicide victim sends "avenging spirits" and "defilement" upon those who do not avenge him. The prosecutors warn the jurors that they will suffer from these "avenging spirits" if they do not properly vote for a conviction.[2] A defendant counters this, not by denying the existence or efficacy of "avenging spirits," but by claiming that the failure to obtain conviction lies with the prosecutor, and therefore the prosecutor, and not the jury, would suffer from the "avenging spirits" in case of a wrongful acquittal.[3] We thus have the same religious belief, that "avenging spirits" and "defilement" attend those who do not properly avenge a homicide victim, but it is applied in two different ways.

Andocides had participated in the impious disfigurement of the statues of Hermes in 415, and some years later he was charged with violating a law forbidding sinners from entering the sanctuaries. During the interval he had engaged extensively in seafaring and trade. Andocides argued (1.137–139) that because the gods had not destroyed him amidst the hazards of seafaring, he must therefore not have wronged the gods. The prosecutor (Lysias 6.19–20), to counter Andocides' argument, claimed that the god did not destroy Andocides at sea in order that he might return to Athens and receive his punishment there. Underlying both arguments is the conviction that the gods (or god) punish those who sin against them. Each orator has applied this belief in the way that best suited his immediate purpose.

When in the 330s the legality of the proposal to award Demosthenes a crown for his service to the state was challenged, Demosthenes (18) and Aeschines (3) used the occasion for long and vituperative attacks on each other. The attacks range far and wide, and in the course of these long speeches numerous religious issues are touched upon. Both orators assume that the gods help Athens but that individual men—usually the speaker's opponent—harm her.[4] Aeschines, of course, throughout holds Demosthenes' policies responsible for the loss at Chaeronea, whereas Demosthenes tends to blame fortune, a daimon, or "some god."[5] Both orators assume that the gods give the army victory in battle, and both claim that the outcome of a legal trial is in the hands of the god as well as of the jurors.[6] Both stress the importance and solemnity of the jurors' oath.[7] Demosthenes' responses to Aeschines' implicit or explicit charges of impious acts are most revealing. Aeschines charged that Demosthenes (1) had frustrated the fulfilment of an oath which the Athenians along with the other members of the association administering Delphi had taken concerning some sacred territory there, (2) had sent out the army to Chaeronea after unfavorable omens, and (3) had caused the arrest and death of his host Anaxinus.[8] In his defense Demosthenes nowhere challenges the religious conceptions underlying these charges. He adopted perhaps the best defense available; i.e., he ignored all the religious aspects of the charges. He clearly avoided reminding the jury of the charges of impiety which Aeschines had made.

These instances of common acceptance of religious beliefs are drawn from sources arguing against one another, and therefore demonstrate all the more vividly the general homogeneity and consensus of religious views in this period. There are, of course, instances of differing beliefs, but they are remarkably few for a religious system which entirely lacked canon law or an enforcing authority. Beliefs differ most in the areas in which there was the most uncertainty expressed, for instance in the conceptions of the afterlife.[9] Some concepts, for example of daimons and of fortune, were vague and changing, and occasionally even the same author expresses differing views about them.[10] But in other areas differences concern mostly the specific application of generally held beliefs.

The consensus described in this study encompasses those beliefs which an Athenian citizen thought he could express publicly and for which he expected to find general acceptance among his peers. It is, in a sense, largely the religion of Xenophon, but it is far more than that, because the evidence from other sources indicates that Xenophon's religious beliefs were virtually identical to those of his contemporaries. It is also the religion of the orators, but what is far more important, it is the religion of their audiences. It is the consensus of the publicly acceptable religious beliefs of Athenians of the late fifth and fourth centuries and, as such, it forms, like festivals, rituals, and poetic and philosophic theories, an important component of the religious milieu of Athens in that period.

F O U R T E E N

Some Historical Considerations

It is often claimed that popular religious belief in Athens deteriorated significantly from the fifth century to the fourth century. Martin Nilsson in particular promoted this interpretation
of the historical development of Athenian religion. He expressed his view in statements such as these:

> The criticisms of religious beliefs by the Sophists and the
> improper jests at the expense of the gods by men like
> Aristophanes did their work. . . . The faith of the masses
> was shaken, but it was not destroyed.[1]

> The old gods had been overthrown by criticism; they
> continued to exist only in public policy and in the minds
> of the simple and credulous, whom the discussions of
> their time passed by. The criticism of the gods' arbitrary
> conduct and their offences against justice and morality
> had done its work. Since the gods did not satisfy the de-
> mand that righteousness should be upheld, that they
> should be an expression and an embodiment of divine
> laws, they were set aside.[2]

This deterioration, or regression, of popular religion is generally attributed to the rationalistic criticisms of the myths and
occasionally of cult practices by the Sophists and by dramatists
such as Euripides and Aristophanes. Nilsson lays part of the

blame on what he sees as increased materialization and secularization of public cult by the state for political purposes.[3]

Scholars have enumerated various "symptoms" of the degeneracy of popular religion in the fourth century. Dodds lists (1)
the increased demand for magical healing, particularly through
the cult of Asclepius, (2) the introduction of orgiastic foreign
cults of Bendis, Sabazius, Attis, Adonis, and others, and (3) increased interest in magic as evidenced by the use of the curse
tablets.[4] Nilsson also views the use of "god" and "gods" in the
abstract collective sense as an indication of this decline.[5] He
would add to the list of these symptoms the appearance of personified deities such as Fortune and Democratia.[6]

It is important to note that apart from the use of "gods" in
the collective sense, these symptoms do not appear in the public or legal orations of the period.[7] No speaker identifies himself
as a devotee of an exotic cult.[8] No speaker proclaims himself a
practitioner of what we might term black magic. The only personified deity who appears at all frequently is Fortune, whose
development is described above.[9] We learn of these symptoms
of regression primarily from essentially private materials such
as the curse tablets and from philosophers' criticisms and caricatures of the society about them. The assertion that these
symptoms of degeneracy or regression appeared only at the
end of the fifth century or with significantly greater frequency
in the fourth century is open to question. But even if this is not
questioned, it is clear that the religious practices commonly described as symptoms of deterioration had not yet attained public respectability. A speaker in a public forum did not wish to
identify himself with them.

Two elements of fourth-century popular religion are quite
mistakenly described as symptoms of deterioration. The first of
these is the secularization of public cult. The introduction of
ruler cult into Athens in the last quarter of the fourth century,
as best evidenced by the divine honors and respect given to the
Macedonian Demetrius Poliorcetes in 307 at the expense of the
traditional gods,[10] is clearly such a symptom, but the inclina-

tion towards a cult of rulers can be traced back in Athens only to the time just preceding the death of Alexander.[11] It should by no means be extended to the whole of the fourth century. There is also no political manipulation of religious cult in the first ninety years of the fourth century to compare with such activities in Athens at the time of the Cylonian conspiracy (VII B.C.) and of the tyrant Pisistratus (VI B.C.). The manipulation of cult and oracles for political purposes had a long tradition in Athens, and it appears no more frequent or intense in the fourth century than in the preceding centuries.

The second element is the use of "god" and "gods" in an abstract collective sense. This has been discussed in detail above.[12] The orators and Xenophon do commonly refer to the gods in this abstract and collective manner. But in doing this they are following a convention of Greek religious thought, a convention which can be traced back as far as Homer.[13] In *Le Polythéisme* G. François offers numerous examples of this usage from the beginnings of Greek literature through the fourth century. Even the Homeric heroes, in their conversations with one another, regularly speak of the gods in this abstract and collective manner.[14] The frequent occurrence of this manner of speaking and thinking about the gods throughout Greek literature prevents us from viewing its occurrence in the fourth century as a sign of debased religious belief.[15]

It is beyond doubt that the criticisms of myths and religious practices by the Sophists and by the dramatists such as Euripides and Aristophanes had a major influence on Greek theology and philosophy in the late fifth century and afterwards. They may even have had a significant effect on the religious attitudes of some aristocratic young men, those types who participated in the mutilation of the herms and the profanation of the Eleusinian Mysteries. But one must beware of overestimating the immediate impact of these rationalistic criticisms on the religious attitudes and beliefs of the general populace of Athens.[16]

The conclusion that popular religious belief deteriorated significantly from, say, the mid-fifth to the mid-fourth century is erroneous. The error in understanding the development of Athenian religion has arisen, it seems to me, because scholars have failed to distinguish properly between the differing natures of the sources for our knowledge of religious beliefs in the earlier and later periods.

Our understanding of fifth-century and earlier religious beliefs concerning the nature of the gods and their role in human life is based primarily upon works of poetry. The authors used most commonly for these purposes are Homer, Hesiod, Pindar, Aeschylus, and Sophocles. The sources for the fourth-century religious beliefs are primarily the historian Xenophon and orators such as Demosthenes, Aeschines, Isocrates, and Isaeus. The difference between the sources of the fifth century and those of the fourth century is more than simply one of years. It is a difference between poetry and prose, with all the factors which that difference implies.

The dramatic and lyric poets of the fifth century and earlier generally follow Homer in assuming not only a superhuman but even a "superdivine" narrative posture. The poets know not only all the affairs of men but also all the affairs of the gods. The poets portray in attractive detail the physical and psychological characteristics of the gods. They describe their actions, motives, and even their innermost thoughts. The poets detail which god intervened in each situation and how and why he did so. In these portrayals the poets consciously followed or varied the mythological framework and divine apparatus established in epic poetry. For our purposes the decisive factor, and that in which the poets differ most from the orators and Xenophon, is that the poets adopted a narrative position of omniscience concerning divine matters. With the orators and Xenophon the situation is quite different. For them to have claimed omniscience in human or divine matters would have been ludicrous. They speak from the human level, as one human being to others. They see some situations and events for which they assign to the gods partial or full responsibility, but they claim little knowledge of and show little interest in the causes or mechanics of divine intervention. They speak in very general and

collective terms about the gods, and they reveal a distinct dis-
inclination, outside cult contexts, to assign specific roles and
personalities to individual gods. This difference between the
highly detailed and fully anthropomorphic conception of the
gods seen in the poets of the fifth century and the collective,
generalized conception of the gods found in the fourth-century
sources is primarily, I think, a difference of genre and does not
reflect a change in religious conceptions.

What we would most welcome, of course, is a collection of
political and forensic orations of the fifth century to compare
to those of the fourth century. We then could compare sources
of like character in order to detect similarities and changes in
popular religious belief. No such corpus of orations from the
fifth century survives.[17] Likewise no dramatic and lyric poetry
of similar character survives from the fourth century to compare to that of the fifth century. It is wrong, I think, to create a
picture of fifth-century religion from strictly poetic sources and
to create a picture of fourth-century religion from strictly prose
sources, and then to claim from a comparison of the two that
there had been a major change in religious attitudes. Such a
comparison will always lead to the disparagement of popular,
"prosaic" religion in the fourth century.

This lack of abundant sources of a similar character will always make analysis of the historical development of Athenian
religious beliefs and attitudes difficult and more subjective than
we might like. A proper study of this topic lies well beyond the
purpose of this book, but I would mention, without elabora-
tion, some possible approaches.

Some evidence indicates that the Athenians were as much
devoted, if not more so, to their religious cults in the fourth
century as they had been in the fifth century. After the disasters
of the Peloponnesian War and the loss of her empire Athens
could no longer afford to build grand temples, but apart from
this, the Athenians continued to devote considerable attention
and money to religious cults and festivals. Nicomachus, a major figure in the recodification of Athenian laws in the last dec-
ade of the fifth century, was accused of introducing into the

state program of religious activities *new* sacrifices costing an additional 36,000 drachmas (Lysias 30.17–20). These sacrifices, so far as we know, were continued throughout the fourth century. The detailed descriptions of ritual and of provisions for festivals,[18] and the numerous calendars of sacrifices also indicate that the Athenians showed no lack of diligence in the celebration of religious festivals and other cult activities in this period. Some critics of the time charged that many state festivals and sacrifices were performed more to satisfy the public's taste for roast meat than for religious reasons,[19] but such criticisms were current and familiar in the fifth century also.[20] Criticisms of this type are to be expected in any age, and they seem no more numerous, intense, or effective in the fourth century than in the fifth.

Sacred calendars, religious dedications, and decrees honoring individuals for religious services are far more numerous from the fourth than from the fifth century. It would be impracticable to do a comparative study of all this epigraphical material here, but to choose one group of evidence, the dedications made by private individuals to the gods offer a reasonably representative sample of the epigraphical evidence and also suggest the complexities of the analysis of this type of material. From the collections of these dedications in *IG* I² 401–837 and *IG* II² 4318–4880 it appears that with the exception of dedications to Athena, more private dedications to deities survive from the fourth century than from all other periods (sixth and fifth, third, second, and first centuries) combined. This is true also of dedications to Olympian deities; with the exclusion of Athena, more private dedications to Olympian deities survive from the fourth century than from all other periods combined.

With Athena the case is somewhat different. Dedications made to Athena by private citizens and erected on the Acropolis reflect this. These dedications are included in *IG* I² 463–759 (before 405/4) and *IG* II² 4318–4350. *IG* I² 463–759 together with newly discovered texts and fragments have been edited by A. Raubitschek, *Dedications of the Athenian Acropolis* (Cambridge, Mass., 1949). Raubitschek has published 393 texts, of

which 84 are indisputably dedications of private individuals to
Athena. Raubitschek dates nearly all of these, usually on the
basis of letter forms, from 525 to 480. Of the 84 only 10 are
dated after 480, and only half of these (nos. 125, 131, 133, 140,
and 218) are dated as late as the mid-fifth century. No dedication is dated later than mid-fifth century. In his study Raubitschek has included all certain dedications by private individuals
recorded in *IG* I² 463–759. If we assume that Raubitschek's
dating of these dedications is correct, it would appear that
there is a complete lack of preserved marble dedications by individuals to Athena from the mid-fifth century until the beginning of the fourth century, because no one of the 22 certain
dedications to Athena listed in *IG* II² 4318–4343 is dated before the fourth century. There are 19 certain dedications to
Athena by private citizens from the fourth century. There are
no dedications from the third, one from the second or first, and
two (*IG* II² 4341, 4347) from the imperial period.[21]

The sequence of dedications by private citizens to Athena
thus seems to have two major lacunae: (1) from mid-fifth century to the beginning of the fourth century and (2) from the
end of the fourth century to the Roman period. The first la-
cuna is very suspicious and may result from Raubitschek's
methods of dating fifth-century dedications. It may be that formal dedications to Athena maintained archaic letter forms as a
matter of style and that thus the method of dating on the basis
of these letter forms is in this case invalidated. We must assume
this, or else that the popular interest in the Athena cult as
expressed in private dedications ceased during the period of
Athens' greatest prosperity and great despair, and that this interest then revived in the fourth century. Whatever the case, the
points of particular importance for this study are that dedications to Athena by private individuals are prevalent in the
fourth century and that they cease to appear only at the end of
the fourth century. The cult of Athena thus continued to win
popular support in the form of private dedications throughout
the fourth century.

The epigraphical evidence thus suggests that the Athenians

of the fourth century devoted themselves to cults and festivals as much as, if not more than, their ancestors of the fifth century. Such evidence, however, might be deceptive. The number of inscribed dedications which survive from any given period depends on many factors besides the religious attitudes of the society. Chance plays a large part in the physical survival of the stones. Varying economic conditions would have determined the possibility of an individual erecting these expensive monuments. Apart from these and similar variables, it could also be argued with some justification that such evidence tells us little of the "quality" of religious beliefs in the period. The same or increased participation in cult activities need not necessarily reflect the same or increased conviction of religious beliefs. All of these factors must be weighed, but it also must be stressed that here, where we have evidence of the same character for both the fifth and fourth centuries, there is no sign of lessening of interest in traditional cult activity in the fourth century.

A second approach to an understanding of the development of Athenian religion in the fifth and fourth centuries, and one which might shed some light on the "quality" of religious belief, would be the bridging of the gulf which lies between the poetic sources of the fifth century and the prose sources of the fourth. Theoretically this would involve (1) a study of poetic and theoretical concepts of the fifth-century sources in the prose sources for popular religion in the fourth century, and (2) a study of popular religious elements gleaned from the fourth century as these elements appear in fifth-century poetry. The first study, the investigation of poetic, mythological, and theoretical elements in fourth-century prose sources for popular religion, holds little promise. As the previous discussions indicate, the Athenians on an everyday, public basis seemed to devote little attention to this aspect of their religious heritage. The second study, tracing the elements of fourth-century popular religion in the fifth-century poets and philosophers, does appear promising. The fifth-century authors' views of these various elements, that is, whether they view them as traditional or innovative, whether they treat them as widely accepted or idiosyncratic, and whether they promote or oppose them, would contribute somewhat to our understanding of their development in Athens in the classical period. It is to this subject that I shall be devoting further work, and I have introduced the topic here only to suggest that it may well be erroneous to disparage the popular, "prosaic" Athenian religion of the fourth century on the basis of what we know of the "poetic" religion of the fifth century.

NOTES

CHAPTER I

1. Fustel de Coulanges, *Ancient City*, 150–151, 201 ff.; Wilamowitz, *Glaube*, 1:1, 2:81; Gernet and Boulanger, *Génie*, 302–303; Adkins, "Greek Religion," 378–379; Burkert, *Griechische Religion*, 191–193.

2. Wilamowitz, *Glaube*, 1:1.

3. For the risks involved in assuming different religious beliefs in different social strata, see den Boer, "Aspects of Religion," 4, 9–11.

4. Nilsson, *Greek Folk Religion*, 5–41, 85.

5. Guthrie, *Greeks and Their Gods*, 258.

6. Dover has written at length, *Popular Morality*, 1–22, on the value of orators, dramatists, and historians as sources for popular morality. His conclusions about these sources may be profitably applied to the topic of popular religious beliefs. The few but important points in which I differ from Dover will be apparent.

7. See, e.g., Meuss, "Vorstellungen," 445–446; Campbell, *Religion in Greek Literature*, 303; Earp, *Way of the Greeks*, 11; Adkins, "Greek Religion," 382; Rudhardt, *Notions*, 6; Dover, *Popular Morality*, 5–6; Wevers, *Isaeus*, 94–121.

8. See Douglas M. MacDowell, *Aristophanes, Wasps* (Oxford, 1971), 3–4, 10–11, 162, 173, 275–276.

9. Dover, *Popular Morality*, 34–35, suspects that the jurors, for the most part, were prosperous men for whom the small pay was only an "honorarium"; but see John H. Kroll, *Athenian Bronze Allotment Plates* (Cambridge, Massachusetts, 1972), 261–263, and A. W. H. Adkins, *CP* 73 (1978), 156–157.

10. Earp, *Way of the Greeks*, 11.

11. Dover, *Popular Morality*, 8–10.

12. For a discussion of this problem see Dover, *Popular Morality*, 4.

13. See Rudhardt, *Notions*, 6; Dover, *Popular Morality*, 17–18. Although Dover well recognizes the difficulties of using the tragedies as evidence, he makes extensive use of them particularly in his discussions of religious topics.

14. See, e.g., Lacey, *Family*; des Places, *Religion grècque*, 229.

15. See Dover's excellent discussion, *Popular Morality*, 18—22. He is, however, more willing than I to accept Aristophanic evidence.
16. Guthrie, *Greeks and Their Gods*, 258—259.
17. See R. Walzer, "Sulla religione di Senofonte"; Kern, *Religion der Griechen*, 3:13—14; Nilsson, *GGR* I³ 791, and *Greek Folk Religion*, 123; Earp, *Way of the Greeks*, 45; Guthrie, *History of Greek Philosophy*, 3:334; Lloyd-Jones, *Justice of Zeus*, 133; J. K. Anderson, *Xenophon* (London, 1974), 34—40.

CHAPTER 2

1. Sacrifices and fumigations: Aeschines 1.22—23 and schol.; schol. to Ar. *Ach.* 44; Dem. 54.39; see Jacoby on *FGrHist* 334 F 16. Heralds' prayers: Aeschines 1.22—23; cf. the prayers which the women and their herald make to open their "ecclesia" in Ar. *Th.* 295—371.
2. Aeschines 1.22—23; Arist. *Ath. Pol.* 43.6. See J. E. Sandys, *Aristotle's Constitution of Athens*² (London, 1912), 172—173.
3. On this alliance see Tod, *GHI*, 2:134—138.
4. Isoc. 1.12—13. On stylistic grounds some question the ascription of this essay to Isocrates. See E. Brémond, *Isocrate, Discours*, vol. 1 (Paris, 1928), 109—111.
5. See pp. 99—100, 103.
6. *Ep.* 1.1. The authenticity of this letter was long questioned but now has been convincingly demonstrated by J. A. Goldstein, *The Letters of Demosthenes* (New York, 1968). Cf. Plato *Ti.* 27C.
7. For examples of Athenian curse tablets see pp. 76—77.
8. Cf. Dem. 4.42, 18.192—193, 195; Aeschines 3.133.
9. See pp. 53—62.
10. See pp. 20, 45—48.
11. The state as a whole: Dem. 1.10—11, 4.42, 18.192—193, 195; Xen. *Hell.* 6.5.41. Legal trials: Lycurgus *Leoc.* 1—2, 91—92; Dinarchus 3.14; Dem. 18.249; Aeschines 2.180. Agriculture: Xen. *Oec.* 17.2; Isoc. 7.29—30.

CHAPTER 3

1. On this general topic see Rudhardt, *Notions*, passim; Dover, *Popular Morality*, 133—138; Burkert, *Griechische Religion*, 396—402.
2. Dem. 1.10—11, 2.1—2, 4.42, 15.2, 18.153, 195, *Prooem.* 24.3; Dinarchus 3.11.
3. Dover, *Popular Morality*, 130.
4. In addition to references in note 2 above, see Aeschines 3.57, 130; Dem. 19.297—299.
5. Dem. 1.10—11; Xen. *Hell.* 6.5.41.
6. Dem. 3.26; [Dem.] 43.66; Xen. *Hell.* 3.14.18, *Ana.* 3.2.10, *Vect.* 6.2—3; Lysias 30.17—20; Antiphon 2.1.10—11; Plato *Lg.* 8.828A—C.

7. Oaths: Dem. 3.26; Lycurgus *Leoc.* 127; Xen. *Ana.* 3.2.10. Sacrifices: Aeschines 3.108–111; Lysias 30.17–20; Antiphon 6.45; [Dem.] 43.66, 59.92; *IG* II² 334; Plato *Lg.* 5.738B–C, 8.828A–C. Pollution from homicide: Antiphon 2.1.10–11, 2.3.9–11, 3.1–2, 4.3.7 (see also pp. 50–52 below); Dem. 23.43.

8. Xen. *Vect.* 6.2–3; Aeschines 3.130; Antiphon 5.81–83; [Dem.] 43.66; *IG* II² 204, lines 23–54; *SEG* 21, no. 519, lines 1–17; Plato *Lg.* 8.828A–C.

9. On religious practices associated with war see Popp, *Einwirkung*, 1–74; W. K. Pritchett, *War*, vol. 3; R. Lonis, *Guerre et religion en Grèce à l'époque classique.*

10. The belief that the gods granted victory in battle can be found throughout Xenophon's writings, as, e.g., in *Ana.* 3.2.7, 5.2.24, 6.5.23, *Hell.* 4.4.12, 7.5.12–13. This belief is also explicit or implied in Lys. 2.58; Isoc. 7.10; Aeschines 3.88; Dem. 4.45, 18.192–194, 216–217, 289–290, 19.130; Ar. *V.* 1085. Cf. Peek, *GV* no. 21. On daimons and fortune: Dem. 18.192–194, 207, 300, 306; Dinarchus 1.93; see also pp. 58–60 below.

11. Pritchett, *War*, 3:11–46, lists forty-nine instances, described by nonpoetic but not necessarily contemporary sources, in which gods or heroes appeared on the battlefield. Only five of these "occurred" in the late fifth and fourth centuries: (1) the Dioscuri to Spartans at Aegospotami in 405 (Plut. *Lys.* 12.1); (2) Zeus Ammon to the Spartan Lysander at Aphytis of the Chalcidice in 403 (Pausanias 3.18.3; Plut. *Lys.* 20.5–6); (3) Heracles (Xenophon *Hell.* 6.4.7) and the Messenian hero Aristomenes (Pausanias 4.32.4) at the battle of Leuctra in 371; (4) the Dioscuri to Jason of Thessaly ca. 370 (Polyaenus 6.1.3); (5) Asclepius to Isyllus (who reported it to the Spartans) (*IG* IV² 128, lines 57–78) in 338. No instance of a deity appearing to an Athenian army is reported for this period. Xenophon himself, who believes in divine influence in matters of war, speaks of some skepticism concerning the reported epiphany of Heracles at Leuctra.

12. Xen. *Ana.* 3.2.8–10, *Hell.* 2.4.14–15, 4.4.12, 5.4.1; Lycurgus *Leoc.* 82; [Dem.] 11.2.

13. Xen. *Oec.* 5.19–20, *Ana.* 3.1.17–18, 3.2.8–9, 4.8.36–39, 6.5.21; Isoc. 14.60; Aeschines 3.131, 152. See Pritchett, *War*, vol. 3, passim.

14. Xen. *Ana.* 6.4.12–22; cf. *Hell.* 3.1.17–19.

15. See pp. 39–49.

16. Cf. Ar. *Pax* 1320–1328; Lycurgus frag. 6 (Burtt).

17. Xen. *Oec.* 17.2, 20.11; Isoc. 7.29–30, 11.13; *IG* I² 94, line 34; Ar. *Nu.* 365–368, *Pax* 1140–1158, *Av.* 1592–1593, *V.* 260–261, schol. to *Ach.* 171.

18. Xen. *Oec.* 17.2; Isoc. 7.29–30.

19. Xen. *Vect.* 1.3–5. Cf. Xen. *Ana.* 5.3.4–13; Dem. 21.51–53; Isoc. 4.28; Lycurgus frag. 4.2 (Burtt).

20. Curses on produce: Aeschines 3.108–111 and the oath (Tod, *GHI*, vol. 2, no. 204, lines 39–46) which the Greek forces, including the Athenians, allegedly swore before the battle of Plataea in 479. This oath, recorded on an inscription of IV B.C., may be a forgery. See G. Daux, Χαριστήριον εἰς ᾽Α.

K. Ὀρλάνδου, vol. 1 (Athens, 1965), 86–87. Pollution from homicide: Antiphon 2.2.10–11. The belief that the pollution of homicide harmed agricultural success may have been obsolete by IV B.C. See pp. 50–52. First-fruit offerings: Xen. *Symp.* 4.47–49, *Ana.* 5.3.4–13; Porph. *Abst.* 4.22.

21. Lycurgus frag. 4.2 (Burtt); Ar. *Eq.* 729 and schol.; schol. to Ar. *Pl.* 1054; Suda s.v. εἰρεσιώνη II. See also Nilsson, *GGR* I³ 122–126, and *Greek Folk Religion*, 36–40.

22. Lycurgus frag. 4.2 (Burtt); schol. to Ar. *Lys.* 645. On these scholia see W. Sale, *RhM* 118 (1975), 265–284.

23. See, e.g., Ar. *Av.* 586–610, where the Hoopoe, incredulous that the birds might replace the gods, is told by Peisthetaerus how the birds could provide to men success in agriculture (588–591), wealth (593–601), health (603–605), and a ripe old age (606–609). In 729–736 the birds promise to men health and wealth, happiness, life, peace, youth, laughter, dances, feasts, and birds' milk. Cf. 878 and 1101–1117.

24. The distinction between "preventive" and "curative" medicine would probably have been intelligible to the Athenians. Their gods involved in medical matters seem to have belonged to one aspect or the other, but not to both. Athena Hygieia and Zeus Ktesios, e.g., were asked to give good health (*IG* II² 334; Isaeus 8.15–16) but did no healing, whereas Asclepius was usually invoked only in times of ill health.

25. See Nilsson, *Greek Folk Religion*, 93–95.

26. Plato *Lg.* 10.909E–910A. On the nature of these votive gifts to healing deities see Rouse, *Votive Offerings*, 208–227.

27. *IG* II² 4400, a father for his children; 4351, for a son; 4372, for a wife; 4403, for children; 4588, for a child; 4593, for a daughter.

28. *IG* IV² 121, lines 33–41. For descriptions of numerous miraculous cures by Asclepius, like the cure of Ambrosia's blindness, see the translation of *IG* IV² 121–122 in L. and E. Edelstein, *Asclepius*, 1:221–237.

29. See pp. 18–21.

30. Rouse, *Votive Offerings*, 95–148; Pritchett, *War*, 3:186–189.

31. Rouse, *Votive Offerings*, 109–110, 116, 138–140; Pritchett, *War*, 3:248–269.

32. Aeschines 3.108–111; [Xen.] *Ath. Pol.* 2.6; Dem. 54.40–41.

33. *IG* II² 4334. Cf. *IG* II² 4337, 4339; *SEG* 17, no. 79.

34. Cf. Ar. *Pl.* 132–134, 1124–1125, 1171–1184.

35. Cf. Xen. *Eq. Mag.* 1.1, 3.1; Aeschines 1.133–134.

36. [Dem.] 43.12. Cf. Xen. *Oec.* 7.12; Aeschines 3.111; Ar. *Pax* 1325.

37. Lysias 32.13; Dem. 54.40–41. Cf. Lysias 12.9–10; Dem. 19.292, 23.67, 29.26, 33, 54, 59.10; Aeschines 3.111; Andocides 1.31, 98, 126; Lycurgus *Leoc.* 79; Ar. *Th.* 332–367, *Ra.* 586–588.

38. Aristophanes (*Th.* 286–291) has Mnesilochus, who is disguised as a matron at the religious festival of the Thesmophoria, pray to Demeter and Persephone to give his daughter a rich and simple husband and his son some good sense.

39. On Andocides and this affair see MacDowell, *Andokides*, 1–18.
40. Cf. Dem. 32.8.

CHAPTER 4

 1. Lycurgus *Leoc.* 1–2, 91–92; Dinarchus 1.98, 3.14. On treason as sacrilege see pp. 94–95 below.
 2. Guilt for impious acts: Lycurgus *Leoc.* 146; [Dem.] 59.109; Lysias 6.13. For murder: Antiphon 2.3.9–11, 4.1.2–4.
 3. See pp. 91–93.
 4. Aeschines 3.108–111 and the following curse tablets: Wünsch, *Defixionum Tabellae* nos. 38, 39, 47–50, 65, 66, 95, 103; E. Ziebarth, *Nachrichten der Gesellschaft der Wissenschaft zu Göttingen* 1899, 105–133, no. 6; Peek, *Kerameikos*, vol. 3, 89–100, no. 4.
 5. Plea for good sense: Dem. 18.1–2, 8. Credit for victories: Dem. 18.249. Prayer for success: Dem. 18.1–2, 8, 141; Aeschines 2.180; [Demades] 1.2; Hyperides 1, frag. 3 (Kenyon).
 6. Evidence of guilt or innocence: Antiphon 5.81–83; Andocides 1.137–139. Bringing the guilty to justice: Andocides 1.114, 137–139; Lysias 16.19–20, 22, 27, 31–32.
 7. Dem. 19.239–240; Lycurgus *Leoc.* 146; Lysias 6.53; [Dem.] 59.126. Punishment for unjust voting: Antiphon 2.3.9–11, 4.1.2–4; Lycurgus *Leoc.* 146; Lysias 6.13; [Dem.] 59.109.
 8. Dover, *Popular Morality*, 255.
 9. Dover, *Popular Morality*, 255.
10. Dover, *Popular Morality*, 255.
11. Dionysius of Halicarnassus (*Dem.* 57) questioned Demosthenic authorship of the speech. See also A. Schaefer, *Demosthenes und seine Zeit*, vol. 3.2 (Leipzig, 1858), 113–129; F. Blass, *Die Attische Beredsamkeit*,[2] vol. 3.1 (Leipzig, 1893), 408–417; F. Graf, *Eleusis und die orphische Dichtung Athens in vorhellenistischer Zeit* (Berlin, 1974), 31, n. 42. G. Mathieu, *Démosthène, Plaidoyers politiques*, vol. 4 (Paris, 1947), 129–138, supports Demosthenic authorship.
12. It may be appropriate here to paraphrase Dover, *Popular Morality*, 10, and note that it is remarkable how often, when in our reading of the orators a passage strikes us as sophisticated, intellectual, artificial, or otherwise unusual, the speech in question turns out to belong to one of the categories of speeches which was never intended to be presented to a legal or legislative assembly.
13. Cf. Burkert, *Griechische Religion*, 374.
14. This interpretation is at odds with, to give an extreme, that of Lloyd-Jones, *Justice of Zeus*, 109, who claims that "from the time of Hesiod to the collapse of paganism, it is generally true that anyone who believed in the exis-

tence of the gods believed that they were just and righteous." Adkins, *Merit and Responsibility*, 255, is closer to the mark in his claim that the Athenians of the classical period no longer believed "that the gods punish injustice," if, of course, we except acts of injustice which simultaneously involved acts of impiety. Dover's treatment of the role of the gods in human justice, *Popular Morality*, 255–261, depends on much evidence which is of doubtful value for popular religious beliefs and popular morality in Athens. For more general discussions of the role of Greek gods in human justice see Earp, *Way of the Greeks*, 69–70; Nilsson, *Greek Folk Religion*, 107; Guthrie, *Greeks and Their Gods*, 121.

CHAPTER 5

1. On the religious aspects of oaths see K. Latte, *RE* 15 (1931), cols. 346–353; Rudhardt, *Notions*, 202–212; Plescia, *Oath and Perjury*; Dover, *Popular Morality*, 250–252.
2. The representative sent by Athens to the international council which administered Delphi.
3. The text of this oath is preserved in the manuscript of Demosthenes 24. The text may not be strictly authentic and lacks certain elements thought to be part of the authentic oath: see Harrison, *Law of Athens*, vol. 2, 48; Plescia, *Oath and Perjury*, 26–29. The text does seem, however, to present in general outlines and in several details the jurors' oath of IV B.C.
4. Arist. *Ath. Pol.* 55.5, 7.1; Plut. *Solon* 25.2; Pollux 8.86.
5. For the text of this oath, preserved in a IV B.C. inscription, see Tod, *GHI*, vol. 2, no. 204. Cf. Dem. 19.303; Lycurgus *Leoc.* 76–78; Stobaeus *Florilegium* 43.48; Pollux 8.105–106.
6. Aeschines 3.108–111; the oath sworn at Plataea, Tod, *GHI*, vol. 2, no. 204, lines 39–46.
7. Xen. *Ana.* 2.5.5–7, 3.2.8–10, *Ages.* 3.1–5.
8. Demes were small, originally regionally determined political units, numbering about 139. In the fifth and fourth centuries membership, which was tantamount to full citizenship in the state, was hereditary but was also subject to the scrutiny of fellow demesmen. See Arist. *Ath. Pol.* 42.1; Isaeus 7.28; Dem. 57.61. The phratries were "brotherhoods" to which families as a group belonged. Membership, like that in the demes, was hereditary but ultimately decided by fellow members. In this period the phratry had some religious activities, but its major function was to establish, by membership, the legitimacy of male offspring. See [Dem.] 43.13–14; *IG* II^2 1237. See Roussel, *Tribu et cité*, 139–151. A genos was a "clan," the member families of which traced their descent from a putative common ancestor. Isaeus 7.15–16; Andocides 1.127; [Dem.] 59.60. For the nature and history of Athenian gene see MacKendrick, *Athenian Aristocracy*; Roussel, *Tribu et cité*, 65–78.

9. Dem. 23.67–68; Aeschines 2.87; Antiphon 6.4–6. On these oaths see Mac-Dowell, *Athenian Homicide Law*, 90–100.

10. Cf. the oath sworn at Plataea, Tod, *GHI*, vol. 2, no. 204, lines 39–46.

11. Dem. 19.239–240, 292, 23.67–68, 24.149–151, 29.26, 33, 54, 54.40–41; Aeschines 2.87; Andocides 1.31, 98, 126; Lysias 12.9–10, 32.13; Ar. *Ra.* 586–588.

12. General prosperity: Dem. 3.26; Lycurgus *Leoc.* 127. Help in war: Xen. *Ana.* 3.2.10, *Hell.* 5.4.1; Lycurgus *Leoc.* 82; [Dem.] 11.2; *IG* II² 97, lines 24–26. Hopes for the future: Dem. 19.239–240; Aeschines 2.87; Lysias 6.53; Lycurgus *Leoc.* 79; Isoc. 18.3.

13. Dem. 19.239–240, 292, 23.67–68, 24.149–151, 29.26, 33, 54, 54.40–41; [Dem.] 59.10; Aeschines 2.87, 3.111; Andocides 1.31, 98, 126; Lysias 12.9–10, 32.13; Ar. *Ra.* 586–588.

14. See Glotz, *Solidarité de la famille*, esp. 557–576.

15. Aeschines (2.158) hyperbolically described Demosthenes as an "avenging spirit" which could, in a Hesiodic manner, bring destruction upon the entire city. Lysias (6.19–20) in his attack against Andocides claims to have seen descendants punished for the impieties of their ancestors and Plato (*Rep.* 2.364B–C) describes individuals who seek purifications and expiations for crimes their ancestors may have committed. Such notions of group or family responsibility for the misbehavior of individual members were obviously familiar to the Athenians, but they occur so infrequently in our sources that one doubts that they were widely accepted.

16. Lysias 32.13; Dinarchus 3.2; Antiphon 6.39; Isoc. 17.15; Isaeus 2.31–32, 12.9; Dem. 36.15–16, 40.11. See Rudhardt, *Notions*, 202–204; Dover, *Popular Morality*, 257.

17. See Plescia, *Oath and Perjury*, 40–57.

18. Isaeus 7.15–16; *IG* II² 1237.

19. Cf. Plato *Rep.* 2.364B–365A, *Lg.* 10.885B, 905D–907B.

20. For a comic treatment of this concept see Ar. *Av.* 1606–1613.

21. Isoc. 1.12–13; Xen. *Symp.* 4.47–49.

22. Antiphon 6.33, 48; Dem. 3.26; Xen. *Hell.* 2.4.42.

23. See Burkert, *Griechische Religion*, 381–382.

CHAPTER 6

1. On Greek divination in general see Halliday, *Greek Divination*; Defradas, "Divination en Grèce"; Nock, "Religious Attitudes" = *Essays*, 534–550; Pritchett, *War*, vol. 3.

2. Of sacrifices: Xen. *Oec.* 5.19–20, *Vect.* 6.2–3, *Ana.* 4.3.8–9, 6.2.15, 6.4.12–22, 6.5.21, 7.8.1–6; Dem. 21.51–53; [Dem.] 43.66; Arist. *Ath. Pol.* 54.6–8; Suda s.v. δεκάτην ἑστιᾶσαι. Of omens: Xen. *Oec.* 5.19–20, *Vect.* 6.2–3, *Mem.* 1.1.2–3, *Ana.* 3.2.8–9, 6.5.21; [Dem.] 43.66; Aeschines 3.130; Theophrastus *Char.* 16. Of voices, if we assume that Xenophon means by this

"oracles": Xen. *Vect.* 6.2–3, *Ana.* 3.1.4–8; Dem. 19.297–299, 21.51–53; [Dem.] 43.66; Aeschines 3.108–111, 130; Lycurgus *Leoc.* 93; Hyperides 4.14–15, 24–25 (Kenyon); Plato *Rep.* 4.427B–C, *Lg.* 5.738B–E, 8.828A–C; Arist. *Ath. Pol.* 21.6, 54.6–8; *IG* II² 204, lines 23–54, 4602, 4969; *SEG* 21, no. 519, lines 1–17. Of dreams: Xen. *Eq. Mag.* 9.7–9, *Symp.* 4.47–49, *Ana.* 3.1.11–12, 4.3.8–9, 6.1.20–24; Aeschines 3.77; Hyperides 4.14–15 (Kenyon); Plato *Lg.* 10.909E–910A; Theophrastus *Char.* 16; *IG* IV² 121, lines 33–41.

3. In this period Delphi was the major center of consultation for both the state and individuals: Xen. *Ana.* 3.1.4–8; Dem. 21.51–53; [Dem.] 43.66; Aeschines 3.108–111, 130; Lycurgus *Leoc.* 93; Hyperides 4.14–15 (Kenyon); Plato *Rep.* 4.427B–C, *Lg.* 5.738B–E, 8.828A–C; *SEG* 21, no. 519, lines 1–17; *IG* II² 4969, and 204, lines 23–54. The Athenians directed state enquiries to Zeus at Dodona occasionally: Xen. *Vect.* 6.2–3; Dem. 19.297–299 and 21.51–53; Hyperides 4.24–25 (Kenyon), mostly when political circumstances made Delphi inaccessible or hostile to them. See Parke and Wormell, *Delphic Oracle*, 1:233–243; Parke, *Oracles of Zeus*, 141–143.

4. Cf. Nock, "Religious Attitudes," 476 = *Essays*, 541. In Nilsson's opinion, *Greek Folk Religion*, 123, divination "was the part of religion which was of most current interest" in this period.

5. On the nature of the dreams of the Greeks, and particularly on incubation in healing sanctuaries, see Dodds, *Greeks and the Irrational*, 102–134.

6. On some of the intricacies in interpreting dreams in antiquity see Meier, "Dream in Ancient Greece," 303–319. For an anthology of ancient theoretical writings (some of IV B.C.) on the interpretation of prophetic dreams, see Naphtali Lewis, *Dreams and Portents* (Toronto, 1980). In their fanciful and eccentric constructions some of the ancient theories and manuals of dream interpretation nearly rival current Freudian analysis of similar material; see, e.g., George Devereux, *Dreams in Greek Tragedy* (Oxford, 1976).

7. On chresmologues and manteis see Oliver, *Athenian Expounders*; Fontenrose, *Delphic Oracle*, 145–165; Bouché-Leclercq, *Histoire de la divination*, 2:1–226.

8. E.g., *Ana.* 5.2.9, 5.5.2–3, 5.6.16–18, 29, 6.4.12–22, 7.8.10.

9. M. I. Osborne, *BSA* 65 (1970), 151–174; cf. *SEG* 16, no. 193.

10. Pl. *Rep.* 2.364B–C, *Lg.* 10.909A–910D, 11.933A–E.

11. Pl. *Euthyphr.* 4C; Theophrastus *Char.* 16.6; Isaeus 8.39; Dem. 47.68–71. The exegetes' specific role in state and private religion, their origins, and their number have been the subject of a lively debate. See Oliver, *Athenian Expounders* and *AJP* 73 (1952), 406–413, 75 (1954), 160–174; H. Bloch, *AJP* 74 (1953), 407–418, *HSCP* 62 (1957), 37–49.

12. See Oliver, *Athenian Expounders*, 8–17.

13. *Rep.* 4.427B–C, *Lg.* 5.738B–E and 8.828A–C.

14. Festivals and sacrifices: Dem. 21.51–53; [Dem.] 43.66; Hyperides 4.24–25 (Kenyon); Plato *Rep.* 4.427B–C, *Lg.* 5.738B–E, 8.828A–C. New cults: Arist. *Ath. Pol.* 21.6; Plato *Rep.* 4.427B–C.

15. The prytany was a subcommittee of fifty who, for one-tenth of the year, prepared the agenda for meetings of the boule, the legislative council of five hundred.

16. The eventual response of the god indicated that this sacred land should not be leased and should remain untilled. See Androtion (*FGrHist* 324 F 30) and Philochorus (328 F 155).

17. It is noteworthy that of the 75 Delphic oracles which Fontenrose, *Delphic Oracle*, 27, considers historical, as contrasted to legendary or quasi-historical, 73% concern *res divinae* such as cult foundations (20.3%), sacrifices and omens (31.1%), and religious laws and customs (21.6%); 18.9% concern *res publicae* and only 8.1% concern *res domesticae*.

18. Xenophon personally: *Ana.* 3.1.11–12, 3.1.4–8, 6.1.20–24, 6.2.15. His army: *Ana.* 3.2.8–9, 4.3.8–9, 6.4.12–22, 6.5.21.

19. See chapter 1, n. 17; Nilsson, *GGR* I³ 791–795.

20. Cf. the criticisms of Nicias in Thuc. 7.50; Plut. *Nic.* 23.1–24.1, *Comp. Nic. Crass.* 5.2.

21. Enneacrounus, the famous Athenian fountain, is only a conjecture here and may be wrong. For this see R. G. Ussher, *The Characters of Theophrastos* (London, 1960), 136. Ussher also provides, 135–157, a multitude of ancient and modern parallels to the practices described throughout this text.

22. Cf. Ar. *Ec.* 792.

23. A Thraco-Phrygian god very similar to Dionysus. He had devotees in Athens at least from the end of V B.C. Cf. Ar. *Lys.* 387–390; Dem. 18.259–260.

24. On the nature of this "holy snake" see Arist. *HA* 607a30–33.

25. On exegetes as "interpreters" or "expounders" of sacred law, see p. 41.

26. On the religious character of these days of the month see Mikalson, *Sacred and Civil Calendar*, 16–19. On the problems of interpretation of this passage see Ussher, *Characters*, 149–150.

27. The Orpheotelestae, "Orpheus' initiators," were itinerant priests who performed Orphic-type initiations for a fee. Cf. Plato *Rep.* 2.364E.

28. On the difficulties of interpretation of the "garlic garland" see Ussher, *Characters*, 154–155.

29. The superstitious man's fears are directed primarily towards pollution, and he practises divination to find the appropriate purification from his imagined pollution. See Bolkestein, *Theophrastos' Charakter der Deisidaimonia*, 72–78.

30. See pp. 103–104.

31. See Gernet and Boulanger, *Génie*, 286.

32. Xen. *Vect.* 6.2–3, *Ana.* 3.1.4–8, 6.2.15; [Dem.] 43.66; *IG* II² 204, lines 23–54; *SEG* 21, no. 519, lines 1–17. See P. Gauthier, *Un Commentaire historique des Poroi de Xénophon* (Paris, 1976), 219.

33. Cf. Rudhardt, *Notions*, 58–59.

34. An omen was, as Nock summarizes it, "Religious Attitudes," 477 = *Essays*,

542, "not so much an indication of inevitable destiny as a token of luck or an endorsement of policy."

35. Cf. Aeschines 3.131. See also Nock, "Religious Attitudes," 473–474 = *Essays*, 536.

CHAPTER 7

1. Fortune: Antiphon 6.15; Dem. 4.12; Dinarchus 1.32–33; Peek, *GV* no. 1698 = *IG* II² 6626, no. 1689 = *IG* II² 7863. A daimon: Xen. *Hell.* 7.4.3; Peek, *GV* no. 1499 = *IG* II² 12974, no. 1783 = *IG* II² 13087, no. 1118 = *IG* II² 13102. Destiny: Peek, *GV* no. 931 = *IG* II² 13098, no. 546 = *IG* II² 6214, no. 1653 = *IG* II² 10435, no. 1909 = *IG* II² 13097, no. 1986 = *IG* II² 7227, no. 2016 = *IG* II² 5673.

2. See pp. 58–60.

3. Cf. Burkert, *Griechische Religion*, 309–312; W. S. Barrett, *Euripides, Hippolytos* (Oxford, 1964), 414; Ehnmark, "Some Remarks on the Idea of Immortality," 8–10.

4. On pollution for acts of homicide see Rohde, *Psyche*, 174–182; Moulinier, *Le Pur et l'impur dans la pensée des Grecs*; Adkins, *Merit and Responsibility*, 86–115; MacDowell, *Athenian Homicide Law*, 141–150. On avenging spirits, see Rudhardt, *Notions*, 53–55, 120–121.

5. Each of the three *Tetralogies* consists of four speeches composed for a hypothetical murder trial. In each tetralogy two of the speeches are for the prosecutor and two for the defendant. These were rhetorical exercises which were written in the sophistic style and which focused on various aspects of legal and religious responsibility for homicide (Adkins, *Merit and Responsibility*, 102–106, 113 n. 26). Whether or not Antiphon himself composed these tetralogies and, if he did, at what date, are extremely difficult and complex questions. Dover, *CQ* 44 (1950), 56–60, concludes mostly on stylistic grounds that if they were composed by Antiphon they must antedate his earliest (ca. 420/19) forensic orations. Cf. Kennedy, *Persuasion*, 129.

6. Cf. Antiphon 2.1.10–11, 2.3.9–11, 3.3.11–12, 4.2.7–9.

7. Rohde, *Psyche*, 176–177, is mistaken, I think, in claiming that at Athens, even in the fourth century, belief in the vengeful soul of the homicide victim and in avenging spirits survived "in undiminished vigour." In the fifth century and earlier, avenging spirits had become a literary topos and in this form they survived throughout antiquity. Traces of earlier belief in them survive in some legal and social practices of the fourth century (see Rohde, *Psyche*, 176–182), but there is no indication of current religious belief in them.

8. Antiphon 2.3.9–11, 3.3.11–12, 6.4–6.

9. Antiphon 2.1.10–11, 3.1.2, 4.3.7; Dem. 23.43.

10. Dem. 20.158. Cf. Antiphon 5.10, 6.4–6; Arist. *Ath. Pol.* 57.4; Plato *Lg.*

9.868A. MacDowell, *Athenian Homicide Law*, 142–146, quite properly notes that Demosthenes (20.158) treats these prohibitions only as a deterrent, and not as a matter of pollution. But Antiphon (2.1.10–11) clearly notes that the murderer pollutes the "purity" of the sacred precincts, and this would explain why the murderer was excluded primarily from religious activities. In any case, MacDowell's point that in the fourth century deterrence, apart from pollution, was a significant factor in these prohibitions is well taken. See below, pp. 86–88.

11. Dem. 20.158, 23.67–68; Aeschines 2.87; Antiphon 6.4–6.
12. For other reasons for the continued importance of pollution, and for an excellent discussion of related points, see Adkins, *Merit and Responsibility*, 92–96, 111 n. 21.

CHAPTER 8

1. Cf. Gernet and Boulanger, *Génie*, 280–281.
2. For other dedications to Asclepius see *IG* II² 4351, 4366, 4372, 4400, 4403, 4415.
3. On Asclepius and his cult see E. and L. Edelstein, *Asclepius*.
4. For a comic description of "medical" treatment at the sanctuary of Asclepius in the Piraeus see Ar. *Pl.* 653–748.
5. See pp. 21, 25–26.
6. See pp. 39–49.
7. Cf. Isoc. 5.149, 15.246–247.
8. Cf. Lysias 6.22, 27, 31–32; Andocides 1.113–114, 117; Dem. 4.42, 9.54, 14.39.
9. See Dover, *Popular Morality*, 259.
10. Cf. Dem. *Prooem.* 25.3; Aeschines 1.116; Xen. *Ana.* 6.1.26.
11. Cf. Dem. 20.25; Lysias 18.18, 21.15.
12. See Dover, *Popular Morality*, 136–137.
13. *Ana.* 3.1.22–23; cf. 3.1.42.
14. Dem. 1.10–11, 2.1–2, 15.2, *Prooem.* 24.3; Dinarchus 3.11; Xen. *Hell.* 6.5.41.
15. Andocides 1.137–139; Lysias 6.19–20; Lycurgus *Leoc.* 91–92.
16. See Meuss, "Vorstellungen," 458–467; Nilsson, *Greek Piety*, 60–61.
17. Cf. Aeschines 2.131; Dinarchus 1.93; Dem. 18.207, 300, 306, *Prooem.* 2.3, 25.2. For similar almost synonymous uses of "the daimon," "the god," and "fortune" see Dem. 1.11, 2.1–2.
18. "The god," "the daimon," and "fortune" are all very similar in this passage, but they are not literally synonymous. In this period one did not say, I think, "the outcome of all things is as fortune wishes it" or "as the god wishes it." Nor would one say that the outcome of a battle was in "fortune's hands." But although these terms are not literally synonymous, Demosthenes has clearly merged them conceptually. On this merging see Dover, *Popular Morality*, 80, 138–141; Rudhardt, *Notions*, 106.

19. The attribution of success to the gods but failure to a daimon or fortune goes considerably beyond the natural inclination, noted by Adkins, "Greek Religion," 382, that the worshiper will "in his prayers and worship emphasize the beneficent aspect of the deity to whom he prays, in the hope that the deity will manifest that facet of himself in his response." We have in our sources virtually no recognition of the harmful aspects of Olympian deities such as appear regularly in, e.g., Greek tragedy.

20. See chapter 3, n. 23 (on Ar. *Av.*); Antiphon 6.15; Dem. 4.12; Dinarchus 1.32–33; Xen. *Hell.* 7.4.3; Peek, *GV* no. 1499 = *IG* II² 12974, no. 1698 = *IG* II² 6626.

21. See G. Herzog-Hauser, *RE* VII (1948), 1643–1689; Nilsson, *Greek Piety*, 85–87; Wilamowitz, *Glaube*, 2:295–305.

22. For fortune in New Comedy see A. W. Gomme and F. H. Sandbach, *Menander* (Oxford, 1973), 74.

23. Dem. 4.12, 45, 9.38, 10.38, 19.55, 317.

24. See pp. 27–30.

25. Meuss, "Vorstellungen," 472–473, sees the orators of the second half of the fourth century, such as Demosthenes, Aeschines, and Dinarchus, making greater use of fortune to explain events than their predecessors had done in the earlier part of the century. But, he notes, these same orators show no less belief than their predecessors in the intervention of the gods. These two fundamentally different ways of viewing the world were evidently able to coexist in the latter part of the fourth century.

26. *IG* II² 333c, lines 19–20, *IG* II² 1496, lines 76–77, 107–108.

27. See Meuss, "Vorstellungen," 470.

28. See Dover, *Popular Morality*, 138–140.

29. See pp. 13–17.

30. Cf. a similar conclusion for the fifth century, drawn by Ed. Fraenkel, *Agamemnon*, vol. 2 (Oxford, 1950), 371–374, primarily on the basis of evidence from tragedy.

CHAPTER 9

1. On the Greek cult of heroes see L. Farnell, *Greek Hero Cults* (Oxford, 1921).

2. Lycurgus *Leoc.* 1–2; Isoc. 14.60; [Dem.] 43.58, 58.14; Plato *Rep.* 4.427B–C, *Lg.* 10.909E–910A; inscription of the Salaminioi in Ferguson, "Salaminioi," 3–5. Although the distinction between gods and heroes is generally valid, there are a number of exceptional cases (some in the calendar of the Salaminioi) in which heroes received sacrifices more characteristic of those usually given to gods. On this, and on the occasional vagaries of the distinction between gods and heroes, see Nock, "Cult of Heroes" = *Essays*, 575–602.

3. Nock, "Cult of Heroes," 171–173 = *Essays*, 599–601, suggests Hecate, the

Erinyes, Hades, and Thanatus as other possible malevolent deities which Isocrates may have had in mind.

4. See discussion and bibliography in Burkert, *Griechische Religion*, 306–312. "Chthonic" is a term which includes "all divine or semi-divine beings supposed to dwell beneath the earth's surface, whether as gods of the dead or of agriculture, as well as the souls of the dead and such heroes as were conceived to dwell under the earth" (J. W. Hewitt, *HSCP* 19 [1908], 63).

5. See Nock, "Cult of Heroes," 164 = *Essays*, 595.

6. Wünsch, *Defixionum Tabellae*, nos. 101, 107; for examples of lead curse tablets, see pp. 76–77.

7. Wünsch, *Defixionum Tabellae*, nos. 87, 89, 95; Peek, *Kerameikos*, vol. 3, 89–100, no. 9 (reproduced here on p. 76).

8. See M. Jameson, *BCH* 89 (1965), 159–166.

9. Plato and his student Xenocrates were largely responsible for the idea of daimons as a distinct class of spiritual beings which was inferior to gods, dangerous, and hostile. Our sources generally do not recognize daimons as a distinct class of deities, but there are a few apparent exceptions in exclamatory statements (Aeschines 3.137; Dem. 42.17; Isaeus 2.47). See Burkert, *Griechische Religion*, 278–282; Gernet and Boulanger, *Génie*, 243–244. For Plato's references to cults of daimons, see *Rep.* 4.427B–C, *Lg.* 8.828A–C, 10.909E–910A.

10. See Jörgensen, "Auftreten der Götter"; Ehnmark, *Idea of God*, 64–73; Nilsson, *Greek Piety*, 59–61; H. J. Rose, "Religion of a Greek Household," 102; Dodds, *Greeks and the Irrational*, 12–13, 23; H. Lloyd-Jones, *Justice of Zeus*, 64.

11. See pp. 58–60, esp. n. 18.

12. Euthias frag. 1 (Müller); Athenaeus 13.590D–591F. For the abundant evidence of Phryne's charms and activities see A. Raubitschek, *RE* 20 (1941), cols. 893–907.

13. On the tendency of Plato and Xenophon to liken Socrates' daimonion to a god, see R. E. Macnaghten, *CR* 28 (1914), 185–189.

14. Cf. Nock, "Cult of Heroes," 145 = *Essays*, 580, "It must of course be remembered that, as Wilamowitz and Nilsson have taught us, the word *daimon* is extremely rare in cult. It is a word of reflection and analysis."

15. See pp. 110–112.

16. Xen. *Oec.* 17.2, 20.11; Isoc. 11.3; *IG* I² 94, line 34; Ar. *Nu.* 365–368, *Pax* 1140–1158, *Av.* 1592–1593, *V.* 260–261.

17. Dem. 19.239–240; Lycurgus *Leoc.* 79; [Dem.] 59.126.

18. See François, *Polythéisme*, passim; Linforth, "Named and Unnamed Gods in Herodotus"; Rudhardt, *Notions*, 103–105; Ehnmark, *Idea of God*, 68–69.

19. For a study of this relationship in Greek literature from Homer to the mid-fourth century see François, *Polythéisme*.

20. See pp. 53–55.

21. See also pp. 59–60, on Dem. 18.192–194.

22. For further examples of the interchangeability of "the gods" and "the god," sometimes even in the same paragraph, see François, *Polythéisme*, 192–200, 213–240.

23. See François, *Polythéisme*, passim; Jones, "Note on ΘΕΟΣ."

24. See Mikalson, "Religion in the Attic Demes." In addition to the excellent original publication of the text by G. Daux, *BCH* 87 (1963), 606–610, see also the restorations proposed by S. Dow, *BCH* 89 (1965), 180–213, and M. Jameson, *BCH* 89 (1965), 156–157.

25. E.g., Dem. 21.51–53; [Dem.] 43.66; *IG* I² 94, *IG* II² 1172, 1199, 1358, 1363; Ferguson, "Salaminioi," 3–5. See Mikalson, "Religion in the Attic Demes"; Solders, *Die ausserstädtischen Kulte*, 1–102.

26. Here and elsewhere the Greek spelling of the epithets of the deities has been maintained. This occasionally allows the epithet's etymological link to the deity's function to be more apparent.

27. For several other mountaintop cults of Zeus in Attica see R. E. Wycherley, *GRBS* 5 (1964), 176 n. 7.

28. Zeus Horios: cf. Plato *Lg.* 8.842E. Zeus Teleios: Pollux 3.37–38; [Dem.] 43.54; schol. to Ar. *Th.* 973. See F. Salviat, *BCH* 88 (1964), 647–654.

29. See M. Jameson, *BCH* 89 (1965), 159–166.

30. Zeus Boulaios: Antiphon 6.45. Zeus Phratrios: [Dem.] 43.13–14; Plato *Euthd.* 302D; Suda s.v. Ἀπατούρια; *IG* II² 1237; Ferguson, "Salaminioi," 3–5.

31. For which see R. E. Wycherley, *The Athenian Agora*, vol. 3: *Literary and Epigraphical Testimonia* (Princeton, 1957), 52.

32. Zeus Herkeios: Arist. *Ath. Pol.* 55.1–3; Dem. 57.66–70; Plato *Euthd.* 302C–D and schol.; Harpocration s.v. ἑρκεῖος Ζεύς; Pollux 8.85–86; *EM* s.v. ἑρκεῖος Ζεύς; Photius s.v. ἑρκείου Διός. Zeus Ktesios: Isaeus 8.15–16; Antiphon 1.16–20; Athenaeus 11.473B–C; Harpocration s.v. Κτησίου Διός.

33. The Greek word for "property" here (*ktesis*) is etymologically linked to Zeus' epithet Ktesios.

34. On the stoa of Zeus see H. Thompson and R. E. Wycherley, *The Athenian Agora*, vol. 14: *The Agora of Athens* (Princeton, 1972), 96–103.

35. See, e.g., Suda s.v. ἐλευθέριος; Harpocration s.v. ἐλευθέριος Ζεύς.

36. On this stoa see Thompson and Wycherley, *Agora of Athens*, 83–90.

37. See chapter 6, note 3. For the Dodonian cult and oracle of Zeus Naios see Parke, *Oracles of Zeus*, 1–163.

38. See note 16 above.

39. Dem. 24.149–151. On at least one occasion the jurors swore their oath by Zeus Basileus (Pollux 8.122).

40. This survey, sufficient for our purposes, does not encompass all the Zeus cults attested for Athens in the various periods. For other Zeus cults, often attested only by boundary stones or isolated literary references, see R. E. Wycherley, *GRBS* 5 (1964), 175–179, and H. Schwabl, *RE* Suppl. 15 (1978), cols. 1064–1078.

41. Cf. Aristophanes' comic treatment of the various epithets of Hermes in *Pl.* 1152–1165.

CHAPTER 10

1. On Greek views of the afterlife see Rohde, *Psyche*, 236–242, 539–544; Rudhardt, *Notions*, 113–126; Adkins, *Merit and Responsibility*, 138–139, 146; Dover, *Popular Morality*, 243–246, 261–267.

2. On Greek epitaphs as sources for religious beliefs see Rohde, *Psyche*, 539–544; Guthrie, *Greeks and Their Gods*, 260–264; Dodds, *Greeks and the Irrational*, 257–258, n. 29; Lattimore, *Themes in Greek and Latin Epitaphs*, 17–20; Clairmont, *Gravestone and Epigram*, 41–71.

3. See pp. 50–52.

4. Cf. Peek, *GV* no. 488 = *IG* II² 5450, no. 1647 = *IG* II² 10998, no. 1697 = *IG* II² 11594, no. 1962 = *IG* II² 12151.

5. See Rohde, *Psyche*, 535–539, nn. 92–93; Lattimore, *Themes in Greek and Latin Epitaphs*, 17.

6. See Nilsson, *GGR* I³ 508–509.

7. The epithet Katochos ("Holder-Down") is related to the purpose of the spell, i.e., "to bind fast."

8. The name Litias could also be written as Littias or Lissias (Peek, *Kerameikos*, vol. 3, 99–100). This man may be the shipbuilder Lissias recorded in *IG* II² 1622, line 316.

9. The name of Galene, a courtesan of some repute (Athenaeus 13.587F), occurs on another tablet, Wünsch, *Defixionum Tabellae*, no. 102.

10. Cf. *BCH* 91 (1967), 515.

11. To Hermes: Wünsch, *Defixionum Tabellae*, nos. 87, 89, 95, 101. To Persephone: Wünsch, nos. 101, 102, 103.

12. For which see Tod, *GHI*, vol. 1, no. 59; Guthrie, *Greeks and Their Gods*, 262–264.

13. See pp. 50–52.

14. Lysias 12.99–100; Dem. 19.66, 20.87; Isoc. 9.2, 14.6, 19.42; Lycurgus *Leoc.* 136.

15. This funeral oration may not have been composed by Demosthenes, but it is clearly of the fourth century. See Kennedy, *Persuasion*, 164–165.

16. Adkins, *Merit and Responsibility*, 200: "funeral orations are not meant to be taken 'au pied de la lettre.'" Cf. Rohde, *Psyche*, 413; Gernet and Boulanger, *Génie*, 371.

17. On rewards and punishments in the afterlife see Rohde, *Psyche*, 236–242; Rudhardt, *Notions*, 113–119; Adkins, *Merit and Responsibility*, 138–148, and "Greek Religion," 409; Dover, *Popular Morality*, 261–267.

18. The relief above this text represents the nurse Melitta seated and a girl standing before her. For a photograph of this relief see *JHS* 36 (1916), 77.

19. Cf. Peek, *GV* no. 1757 = *IG* II² 8870.

20. Cf. Socrates' last words (Plato *Phd.* 118A), "We owe a cock to Asclepius. Give it to him and do not neglect it."
21. See, e.g., Mylonas, *Eleusis*, 267 n. 179.
22. See pp. 36, 104.
23. See pp. 35–36.

CHAPTER II

1. A tribe was one of the ten political units, each having its own eponymous hero, into which the Athenian citizen body was divided. On the nature of demes, phratries, and gene see chapter 5, n. 8.
2. On the general importance of the social or political group in Greek religious worship see Fustel de Coulanges, *Ancient City*, 128; M. N. Tod, *Sidelights on Greek History* (Oxford, 1932), 73; Nilsson, *Greek Piety*, 20; Rudhardt, *Notions*, 109, 289; Gernet and Boulanger, *Génie*, 200, 208; Burkert, *Griechische Religion*, 383–385. The following works treat particularly religious aspects of the various groups:
   Polis: Nestle, *Griechische Religiosität*, 2:9–18; Pfister, "Kultus"; Nilsson, *History*, 240–262; Ehrenberg, *Greek State*, 16–20, 74–77. Tribe: Schlaifer, "Notes on Public Cults," 251–257; Feaver, "Historical Development in Priesthoods," 134–136; Kron, *Phylenheroen*. Deme: Haussoullier, *Vie municipale*, 135–173; Feaver, "Historical Development in Priesthoods," 153–154; Mikalson, "Religion in the Attic Demes," 424–435; Parke, *Festivals*, 175–182. Phratry: Gernet and Boulanger, *Génie*, 297; Guarducci, "Istituzione della fratria"; Jeanmaire, *Couroi et Courètes*, 133–144; Latte, "Phratrie"; Nilsson, *Cults, Myths, Oracles, and Politics*, 150–170; Andrewes, "Philochoros on Phratries." Genos: Toepffer, *Attische Genealogie*; Ferguson, "Salaminioi"; Jeanmaire, *Couroi et Courètes*, 133–144; Feaver, "Historical Development in Priesthoods"; Andrewes, "Philochoros on Phratries"; MacKendrick, *Athenian Aristocracy*; Roussel, *Tribu et cité*, 65–78. Family: Nilsson, *Greek Folk Religion*, 65–83; Lacey, *Family*, 27–28, 147–150.
3. For a general survey of the cults on the Acropolis see B. Jordan, *Servants of the Gods* (Göttingen, 1979), 28–36.
4. On the location of the Pagus in Erchia see E. Vanderpool, *BCH* 89 (1965), 21–24.
5. *IG* II² 1237; Ferguson, "Salaminioi," 3–5.
6. On rites for the dead see Isaeus 2.37, 46, 6.64–65, 9.7; Ar. frag. 488 (Edmonds); Athenaeus 9.409F–410A; Harpocration and Photius s.v. τριακάς; Photius s.v. καθέδρα.
7. On the state cult of these two gods see R. E. Wycherley, *GRBS* 5 (1964), 176–177.
8. On respect for the priority of the gods see pp. 13–17. Introductory purifications, sacrifices, and prayers are best attested for meetings of the eccle-

sia (Aeschines 1.22–23 and scholiast; Dem. 54.39; schol. to Ar. *Ach.* 44; Ar. *Th.* 295–371) and boule (Antiphon 6.45; Dem. 19.190, 21.114–115).

9. Boule: Antiphon 6.45; Dem. 19.190, 21.114–115. Prytany: Isaeus 3.79, 8.18; [Dem.] 43.13–14, 81–82; Pollux 8.107; Theophrastus *Char.* 30.16; Suda s.v. Ἀπατούρια; *IG* II² 1237. Deme: Theophrastus *Char.* 21.11. Phratry: Isaeus 3.80, 6.64, 9.21; Theophrastus *Char.* 10.11–12; Erchia calendar; *IG* II² 1172, 1184, 1187, 1199, 1204, 1214; *SEG* 22, no. 177. Genos: Ferguson, "Salaminioi," 3–5; *IG* II² 1231. Family: Isaeus 8.15–16; Antiphon 1.16–20. Official boards: Dem. 19.190.

10. On the exceptional priesthoods of the eponymous heroes of some tribes see Schlaifer, "Notes on Public Cults," 251–257.

11. Suda and Harpocration s.v. ἀμφιδρομία; Hesychius s.v. δρομιάφιον ἦμαρ; Plato *Tht.* 160D–161A; H. J. Rose, "Religion of a Greek Household," 110–111. Instead of the "parents," the women who delivered the baby may have carried it around the hearth. The evidence is unclear on this point.

12. Suda s.v. δεκάτην ἑστιᾶσαι; Athenaeus 15.668D; Ar. *Av.* 494–495, 922–923; Isaeus 3.30, 70; Dem. 39.20, 22–24, 40.28, 59; Hesychius s.v. δεκάτην θύομεν. Some sources (e.g., Harpocration s.v. ἑβδομευομένου) record a tradition going back to Aristotle (*HA* 588A) and perhaps Lysias that the naming of the child occurred on the seventh day after birth.

13. Schol. to Ar. *Pl.* 768; Theopompus frag. 14 (Edmonds); Dem. 45.74; Lacey, *Family*, 31.

14. On the Apaturia see Herod 1.147; [Dem.] 43.13–14, 81–82; Andocides 1.126; Suda s.v. Ἀπατούρια, and *IG* II² 1237. See also H. T. Wade-Gery, *Essays in Greek History* (Oxford, 1958), 116–134; Andrewes, "Philochoros on Phratries"; and W. E. Thompson, *Symbolae Osloenses* 42 (1968), 51–68.

15. Isaeus 3.79, 8.18; Harpocration s.v. γαμήλια; Erdman, *Die Ehe im alten Griechenland*, 261–266.

16. Isaeus 7.15–16; see Andrewes, "Philochoros on Phratries," 5–6.

17. Admission to the deme: Arist. *Ath. Pol.* 42.1; Isaeus 7.28; Dem. 57.61. To the boule: Lysias 31.1–2; Xen. *Mem.* 1.1.8; see Plescia, *Oath and Perjury*, 25–26. To the archonships: Arist. *Ath. Pol.* 7.1, 55.5; Lycurgus *Leoc.* 79; Plutarch *Solon* 25.2; Pollux 8.86.

18. Tod, *GHI*, vol. 2, no. 204. For the complete text see pp. 33–34 above.

19. See Gernet and Boulanger, *Génie*, 201–202.

20. Cf. Dem. 24.103.

21. See pp. 50–52.

22. Cf. Isaeus 6.49–50.

23. Cf. Aeschines 1.183.

24. As cause of ill-fortune: Antiphon 2.1.10–11; Xen. *Hier.* 4.5; Aeschines 2.158; Plato *Lg.* 9.868A, 9.871A. Endangering the success of rituals: Antiphon 5.81–83.

25. See p. 52.

26. Antiphon 2.3.9–11; Dem. 20.158; [Dem.] 59.85–87; Aeschines 1.183; see MacDowell, *Athenian Homicide Law*, 141–150.
27. Cf. [Dem.] 25.60–62.
28. Cf. Plato *Lg.* 10.909A–910D, 11.933A–E.
29. On Thrasyllus and Sthorys see p. 41.
30. Sacrifices: Xen. *Ana.* 7.8.1–6, *Eq. Mag.* 1.1, 3.1, 5.14; cf. Ar. *Pl.* 133–134, *Pax* 385–389, 416–425. Prayers: Xen. *Ana.* 3.1.22–23, 4.8.25, 6.1.26, *Hell.* 2.4.14– 15, *Mem.* 2.2.10, *Eq. Mag.* 1.1, 3.1, 5.14, *Oec.* 11.8, 20, *Cyn.* 6.13; Dem. 18.1–2, 8, 141, 249, 324, 20.25, 24.7, *Epist.* 1.1, *Prooem.* 25.3; Aeschines 1.116, 133–134, 2.180; Isoc. 8.127, 15.165; Isaeus 8.16; Hyperides frag. 1 (Kenyon); [Demades] 1.2; *IG* II² 4319, 4321 as reedited in *Hesperia* 16 (1947), 287–289; Ar. *Av.* 603, *Pax* 1320–1321, *Pl.* 133–134. On prayers and vows to Asclepius for health see pp. 22–23. Dedications: Lysias 10.39–40; Plato *Lg.* 10.909E– 910A; Theophrastus *Char.* 16.4; Ar. *Pl.* 1179–1180; *IG* II² 4323, 4326, 4334, 4337, 4339, 4357, 4548, 4560, 4602, 4889; *SEG* 17, no. 79, and 23, no. 124. For dedications to Asclepius see chapter 3, n. 33.
31. Xen. *Hier.* 8.3, *Ages.* 8.7, *Hell.* 3.1.24; Isaeus 1.31, 3.79, 8.15–16, 9.21; Antiphon 1.16–20; Isoc. 19.10; cf. Men. *Dysc.* 611–614.
32. Xen. *Hier.* 1.18; Antiphon 1.16–20; [Xen.] *Ath. Pol.* 2.9; Dem. 3.31; Isoc. 7.29–30; Arist. *EN* 8.1160a; Ar. *Nu.* 386–387, 408–409, *Eq.* 652–663.

CHAPTER 12

1. For general discussions of piety and impiety in Greek religion see Nestle, *Griechische Religiosität*, 2:9–18, 62; Earp, *Way of the Greeks*, 69–77; Nock, *Conversion*, 10–18; Gernet and Boulanger, *Génie*, 354–370; Rudhardt, *Notions*, 13–17; Dover, *Popular Morality*, 246–254; Burkert, *Griechische Religion*, 408–412.
2. See J. Rudhardt, *MH* 17 (1960), 87–105; Reverdin, *Religion de la cité*, 208–217; Derenne, *Procès d'impiété*.
3. Arist. *Ath. Pol.* 57.1–2; Dem. 22.27; Hyperides 4.6; cf. Dem. 59.74–77.
4. Introducing a new god: against Phryne, Euthias frag. 1 (Müller); see A. Raubitschek, *RE* 20 (1941), cols. 893–907; against the priestess Ninus, Josephus *Ap.* 2.267; against Socrates, see n. 7 below. Religious revelry: against Phryne, Euthias frag. 1 (Müller); Raubitschek, *RE* 20 (1941), cols. 893–907; and perhaps against Ctesicles, Dem. 21.180. Illegal religious assembly: against Phryne, Euthias frag. 1 (Müller); Raubitschek, *RE* 20 (1941), cols. 893–907. Profanation of Mysteries: against Alcibiades and others, MacDowell, *Andokides*, 1–18; against the Melian Diagoras, L. Woodbury, *Phoenix* 19 (1965), 178–211. Mutilation of herms: against Alcibiades, Andocides, and others, MacDowell, *Andokides*, 1–18.
5. Derenne, *Procès d'impiété*, 258–262.
6. W. Fahr's claim, *Theous Nomizein*, 89–92, that Diagoras the Melian was

prosecuted on the basis of words and thoughts, and not of deeds, may be mistaken. The Athenians would surely have viewed Diagoras' systematic attempt to turn people away from the Eleusinian Mysteries as an impious *act*, and not merely as *talk* arising from a bizarre personal theology.

7. See J. Burnet, *Plato's Euthyphro* (Oxford, 1924), 14–16, 128; C. Phillipson, *The Trial of Socrates* (London, 1928); A. E. Taylor, *Socrates* (New York, 1933; reprinted 1953), 102–129; Fahr, *Theous Nomizein*, 131–157.

8. Diog. L. 2.40; cf. Plato *Ap.*; Xen. *Ap.* 24; *Mem.* 1.1.2–3.

9. See n. 7 above.

10. On Phryne see pp. 65–66.

11. E.g. Xen. *Mem.* 1.1.2–1.1.4, 1.3.1, 1.3.4, *Ap.* 10–11, 24, *Ana.* 3.1.4–8; Plato *Ap.* 21B, 33C, *Phd.* 60D–61B.

12. See pp. 52, 87–88.

13. Antiphon 2.1.10–11, 4.1.2–4, 8–9, 6.4–6.

14. See pp. 50–52.

15. For the text of this oath see pp. 33–34.

16. Dinarchus 1.98, 3.14; Lycurgus *Leoc.* 93.

17. Lysias 2.80; Lycurgus *Leoc.* 88.

18. Arist. *Ath. Pol.* 58.1; Lysias 2.80.

19. See pp. 78–79.

20. Robbing sanctuaries: Xen. *Hell.* 1.7.22; Isoc. 20.6. Chopping down olive trees: Arist. *Ath. Pol.* 60.1–3; Lysias 7; [Dem.] 43.71.

21. *IG* II² 1177, 1362.

22. E.g., Lysias 30.17–20; Isaeus 8.18–19; Isoc. 7.29–30; Lycurgus *Leoc.* 1–2, 97; [Dem.] 43.66, 59.74–77, 85–87, 116; Porphyry *Abst.* 4.22; Arist. *Ath. Pol.* 57.1–2; Plato *Plt.* 290E; *IG* II² 334; Ferguson, "Salaminioi," 3–5.

23. Lysias 30.17–20; Xen. *Mem.* 1.3.1; Lycurgus *Leoc.* 97; [Dem.] 59.74–77; Porph. *Abst.* 2.16; Plato *Lg.* 5.738B–C.

24. Lysias 30.17–20; [Dem.] 59.74–77.

25. E.g., Isaeus 4.19, 6.64–65; Antiphon 6.37; Aeschines 1.13–14, 3.77–78; [Dem.] 43.65–66; Lycurgus *Leoc.* 97. On funeral rites in general see Rohde, *Psyche*, 162–174 and notes; Kurtz and Boardman, *Greek Burial Customs*, 142–161; Alexiou, *Ritual Lament*, 4–23.

26. Third day: Isaeus 2.37; Ar. *Lys.* 611–613 and schol. Ninth day: Isaeus 2.36–37, 8.39; Aeschines 3.225. Thirtieth day: Harpocration and Photius s.v. τριακάς; Photius s.v. καθέδρα. (Alexiou, *Ritual Lament*, 208 n. 38, argues that these rituals should be reckoned from the day of death and not the day of burial.) Annual rituals: Isaeus 2.10, 46, 6.51, 7.30, 9.7; Plato *Lg.* 4.717D–E; Athenaeus 9.409F–410A. For a detailed account of these annual offerings and libations for the dead and of their possible relationship to the festivals of the Genesia and Anthesteria see Wyse, *Speeches of Isaeus*, 269–271.

27. On Zeus Ktesios and Zeus Herkeios, see pp. 70–71. Families erected aniconic pillars or altars of Apollo Agyieus ("Apollo of the Street") in the

streets in front of their house doors. His function was apparently to avert evil from the household. Lycurgus frag. 4.2 (Burtt); Ar. *Pl.* 1054 and schol., *Eq.* 729 and schol.; Harpocration s.v. ἀγυιᾶς; Suda s.v. εἰρεσιώνη. See Nilsson, *GGR* I³ 112–126, and *Greek Folk Religion*, 36–40.

28. See Nilsson, *Greek Piety*, 49.

29. Isoc. 7.29–30; cf. Lysias 30.17–20; Xen. *Mem.* 1.3.1; [Dem.] 59.74–77; Pl. *Lg.* 5.738B–C.

30. See pp. 31–38.

31. Cf. Dover, *Popular Morality*, 249.

32. Plescia, *Oath and Perjury*, 88–91.

33. Wealthy citizens like the speaker were appointed, with the title *choregus* ("chorus-leader"), to pay the expenses for choruses competing in annual state religious festivals such as the Thargelia, Dionysia, and Panathenaia. In this period one drachma was approximately two-thirds of the average daily wage. The speaker continues (21.3–5) to list a further 9,500 drachmas he spent for state religious activities. Cf. Andocides 1.132; Dem. 21.156; Isaeus 7.36; Lycurgus *Leoc.* 139; Xen. *Oec.* 2.5–6.

34. *IG* II² 1187, 1199, 1204, 1214, 1229, 1231; *SEG* 22, no. 177.

35. Cf. Nock, "Religious Attitudes," 479 = *Essays*, 545–546, "A Greek did not scruple to admit the motive of *philotimia*, the desire to make a good show-ing before men, in his liberalities to the gods and their temples. . . . The Greek had no desire to 'Do good by stealth and blush to find it fame.'" Cf. Dover, *Popular Morality*, 180; Bolkestein, *Wohltätigkeit und Armenpflege*, 152–156.

36. *IG* II² 1199, 1231.

37. For discussion of the development of this view among philosophers, see Bolkestein, *Wohltätigkeit und Armenpflege*, 173–177.

38. [Arist.] *VV* 1250b2, 1251a2.

39. See H. Rackham, *Aristotle: The Athenian Constitution, The Eudemian Eth-ics, and On Virtues and Vices* (Cambridge, Massachusetts, 1952), 484–486; Ed. Zeller, *A History of Eclecticism* (London, 1883), 145.

40. Rudhardt, *Notions*, 15.

41. In a section entitled "Extensions of Piety," Dover, *Popular Morality*, 252, claims that in several occurrences of words such as "holy," "unholy," "pious," and "impious," it is "not easy to make any clear connection with religion." He lists instances from the orators in which he claims that these words are applied to dishonesty, illegality, ingratitude, objectionable char-acter, political blackmail, etc. He views this as a "convergence of social and political morality with religion" (253). Such a convergence did undoubtedly occur in some poetic and philosophic writings but not, I think, in popular religion in the manner Dover represents it.

    Dover offers nineteen instances from the orators. Two of these (Aes-chines 3.91; Dem. 57.58) are irrelevant. Most other instances, in the context either of the specific passage or of the speech as a whole, may be better viewed, I think, in terms of the elements of piety discussed above: Isaeus 9.34 in terms of the duty of providing funeral rites; Antiphon 5.7 in terms of the religious aspects of murder; Andocides 1.19, 23, in terms of the respect owed to living parents; Lysias 32.13 and Dem. 33.10, 53.3, in terms of the maintenance of oaths, because oaths surely accompanied financial transactions of the type involved (cf. Dover, 249); Lycurgus *Leoc*. 34, 141, and Dem. 8.8, 18.240, 323, 19.156, in terms of the impiety of treason and of breaking the ephebic oath; and Dem. 21.148 in terms of the sacrilegious behavior of the defendant. In [Dem.] 25.48 "unholy" seems to refer to abandoning the principles of law established by the ancestors, but for the uncertain value of [Dem.] 25 as a source see pp. 29–30 above. The religious context of Dem. 29.39 remains unclear.

"Unholy" and "impious" could also serve as terms of verbal abuse of the type which sprang so easily to the lips of Demosthenes (cf. Dem. 18.240 ff.), and in this case they probably did not require reference to specific action. Aeschines 1.95 seems to be an instance of this type. Some of the occurrences of "unholy" and "impious" listed above may also be of this type, and my attempts (as well as Dover's) to find a specific religious or moral background for each of them may be misdirected. But in any case the orators' very infrequent vague uses of these words do not warrant the assumption of a "convergence of social and political morality with religion" in the popular religious belief of the period.

42. Antiphon 5.81–83, 6.4–6; Xen. *Hell*. 3.4.18, *Ana*. 3.2.10, *Vect*. 6.2–3, *Oec*. 11.7–8; Dem. 3.26, 19.239–240; [Dem.] 11.2, 16; Isoc. 6.59, 7.29–30, 8.33–34, 15.281–282; Lycurgus *Leoc*. 82, 127; *IG* II² 97, lines 24–26. See pp. 18–26, 53–62.

43. See pp. 78–82.

44. Andocides 1.137–139; Lysias 6.1–2, 19–20, 51–53, frag. 73 (Thalheim); Antiphon 2.1.10–11, 2.3.9–11, 4.1.2–4, 8–9, 6.4–6; [Dem.] 59.74–77; Isoc. 8.120; Lycurgus *Leoc*. 93, 129; Xen. *Hell*. 5.4.1; Plato *Lg*. 9.871A; Ar. *Th*. 668–685, 715–716.

45. See pp. 27–30.

46. See P. Maas, *RE* II (1921), cols. 479–481.

47. Cf. Lysias 6.19–20.

48. See Meuss, "Vorstellungen," 456–458.

49. Antiphon 2.1.10–11, 4.1.2–4, 8–9, 6.4–6; Lysias 13.3; Aeschines 3.120–121; Lycurgus *Leoc*. 15; [Dem.] 59.109.

CHAPTER 13

1. The example of the *Tetralogies* is artificial in the sense that these "speeches" were never intended for courtroom presentation. They were all composed by one person whose purpose was, in part, to demonstrate how one could

argue to opposite conclusions from one set of principles and evidence. See chapter 7, n. 5. The following examples from Andocides, Lysias, Demosthenes, and Aeschines are free from this artificiality.

2. 2.1.10–11, 2.3.9–11, 4.1.2–4.

3. 2.1.3, 4.2.8–9.

4. Aeschines 3.57, 129, 196; Dem. 18.153, 195.

5. Dem. 18.192–194, 200, 208, 303, 306.

6. That gods give victory: Aeschines 3.88; Dem. 18.193, 216–217, 290. That gods influence verdicts: Aeschines 3.1; Dem. 18.249, 267.

7. Aeschines 3.233; Dem. 18.2, 7–8, 217, 249.

8. Aeschines 3.108–114, 131, 223–224.

9. See pp. 74–82.

10. See pp. 65–66 (daimons), 58–62 (fortune).

CHAPTER 14

1. *Greek Folk Religion*, 122. Cf. pp. 94, 115; *GGR* I³ 812–815.

2. *Greek Piety*, 78. Cf. pp. 72–78, 116.

3. Nilsson, *Greek Piety*, 66–70, *GGR* I³ 729–734, and *History*, 260–262.

4. Dodds, *Greeks and the Irrational*, 192–195.

5. *GGR* I³ 813, *Greek Piety*, 116.

6. *GGR* I³ 812–815.

7. The religious demeanor of the orators generally provides embarrassment to those who view the fourth century as a religiously debased period. This embarrassment can be avoided only by claiming that the orators do not mean what they say. Nilsson, *Greek Piety*, 77: "They respect the State religion, but at the same time scepticism shows itself in discreet phraseology and shows that fundamentally they shared the general unbelief." Fahr, *Theous Nomizein*, 113: "Die Redner huldigen einerseits der Religion, gleichzeitig lassen sie ihren Skeptizismus in vorsichtigen Wendungen durchblicken und zeigen damit, dass sie im Grunde nicht mehr in dem leben, was sie in ihren Reden hinsichtlich der Religion vertreten." There has yet to be shown an example of such discreet phraseology in the orators.

8. A speaker might, however, with derision portray his opponent as a devotee of a foreign cult. See, e.g., Demosthenes' description of Aeschines' role in the cult of Sabazius (18.259–260).

9. See pp. 58–62.

10. Athenaeus 6.253D–F (on which see Dodds, *Greeks and the Irrational*, 241–242); *SEG* 25, no. 149.

11. See Habicht, *Gottmenschentum und griechische Städte*, 28–36.

12. See pp. 66–68.

13. This convention may even be detected in the Linear B tablets from Cnossus. See Burkert, *Griechische Religion*, 88.

14. See Ehnmark, *Idea of God*, 64–73.

15. Cf. Lloyd-Jones, *Justice of Zeus*, 64.

16. Cf. Gernet and Boulanger, *Génie*, 363–364; A. D. Nock in Nilsson's *Greek Folk Religion*, v–vi; G. S. Kirk, *The Nature of Greek Myths* (Harmondsworth, Middlesex, 1974), 98, 112; Burkert, *Griechische Religion*, 371–372, 452, 473.

17. The speeches in Thucydides' *History* cannot serve as even partial replacement for the wished-for corpus of genuine fifth-century Athenian political and forensic orations. Thucydides may have accurately represented the major policies and concerns of the individuals in whose mouths he placed his speeches, but several factors make those speeches unreliable sources for popular religion. Religious content in speeches is usually encapsulated in casual turns of phrase and offhand comments, and apart from the general difficulty of recalling these over the years, Thucydides' own rhetorical style and his concise presentation of the speeches may have resulted in the loss of these casual phrases concerning religious belief. Because of his own rationalistic and apparently antireligious bias, Thucydides may also have intentionally eliminated religious elements from these speeches.

18. E.g., Arist. *Ath. Pol.* 54.6–8, 60.1–3; Dem. 4.35–36, 21.51–53; Hyperides 4.14–15 (Kenyon); *IG* II² 334, and 204, lines 23–54.

19. Isoc. 7.29–30; Xen. *Hier.* 1.18; Dem. 3.31; Arist. *EN* 8.1160a.

20. [Xen.] *Ath. Pol.* 2.9. In Ar. *Nu.*, Socrates associates "indigestion" with the Panathenaia (386–387), and Strepsiades associates thoughts of cooking with the Diasia (408–409). In Ar. *Eq.* 652–663 two speakers compete for the favor of the boule by proposing increasingly large public sacrifices. It might also be noted that Pericles in the funeral oration (2.38) speaks of contests and sacrifices only as "relaxations from labors" for the mind.

21. *IG* II² 4328, 4329, 4334, and 4339 are all dedications to Athena Ergane ("Worker"). There are no dedications to Athena Ergane from the fifth century (Raubitschek, 88–89), and there is only one reference to her from this period, Sophocles, frag. 760 (Nauck). The question arises whether Athena Ergane is one of the same Athenas (Polias, Parthenos, Pallas) to whom the fifth-century dedications were presented. *IG* II² 4318 would prove that Athena Ergane was Athena Polias if only the restoration were indisputable. The numerous arguments summarized by W. Judeich, *Topographie von Athen* (Munich, 1931), 241–243, suggest, however, that Athena Ergane had a sacred precinct separate from Athena Polias and Athena Parthenos, and thus was a separate cult figure. The regular occurrence of the epithet Ergane in the fourth century, as contrasted to its lack in fifth-century dedications, does suggest a certain change in emphasis in the Athena cult on the Acropolis during the period, but it does not alter the conclusion that her cult received popular support throughout the fourth century.

BIBLIOGRAPHY

Adkins, Arthur W. H. "Greek Religion." In *Historia Religionum*, edited by Claas J. Bleeker and Geo Widengren, vol. 1, 377–441. Leiden, 1969.

———. *Merit and Responsibility*. Oxford, 1960.

Alexiou, Margaret B. *The Ritual Lament in Greek Tradition*. Cambridge, 1974.

Andrewes, Antony. "Philochoros on Phratries." *JHS* 81 (1961), 1–15.

Boer, Willem den. "Aspects of Religion in Classical Greece." *HSCP* 77 (1973), 1–21.

Bolkestein, Hendrik. *Theophrastos' Charakter der Deisidaimonia*. Giessen, 1929.

———. *Wohltätigkeit und Armenpflege im vorchristlichen Altertum*. Utrecht, 1939.

Bouché-Leclercq, Auguste. *Histoire de la divination dans l'antiquité*. 4 vols. Paris, 1879–1882 (reprinted 1963).

Burkert, Walter. *Griechische Religion der archaischen und klassischen Epoche*. Stuttgart, 1977.

———. *Homo Necans*. Berlin, 1972.

Campbell, Lewis. *Religion in Greek Literature*. London, 1898 (reprinted 1971).

Casabona, Jean. *Recherches sur le vocabulaire des sacrifices en Grec*. Aix-en-Provence, 1966.

Clairmont, Christoph W. *Gravestone and Epigram*. Mainz, 1970.

Defradas, Jean. "La Divination en Grèce." In *La Divination*, edited by André Caquot and Marcel Leibovici, vol. 1, 157–195. Paris, 1968.

Derenne, Eudore. *Les Procès d'impiété*. Liège, 1930 (reprinted 1976).

Des Places, Édouard. *La Religion grecque*. Paris, 1969.

Deubner, Ludwig A. *Attische Feste*. Berlin, 1932 (reprinted 1966).

Dodds, Eric R. *The Greeks and the Irrational*. Berkeley, 1951.

———. "The Religion of the Ordinary Man in Classical Greece." In *The Ancient Concept of Progress and Other Essays on Greek Literature and Belief*, 140–155. Oxford, 1973.

Dörrie, Heinrich. "Überlegungen zum Wesen Frömmigkeit." In *Pietas*, edited by Ernst Dassmann and K. Suso Frank, 3–14. Münster, 1980.

Dover, Kenneth J. *Greek Popular Morality*. Berkeley, 1974.

Dow, Sterling. "Six Athenian Sacrificial Calendars." *BCH* 92 (1968), 170–186.

Earp, Frank R. *The Way of the Greeks*. Oxford, 1929.

Edelstein, Ludwig, and Edelstein, Emma J. *Asclepius*. 2 vols. Baltimore, 1945.

Ehnmark, Erland. *The Idea of God in Homer*. Uppsala, 1935.

————. "Some Remarks on the Idea of Immortality in Greek Religion." *Eranos* 46 (1948), 1–21.

Ehrenberg, Victor. *The Greek State*. New York, 1960.

Erdmann, Walter. *Die Ehe im alten Griechenland*. Munich, 1934.

Fahr, Wilhelm. *Theous Nomizein*. New York, 1969.

Farnell, Lewis R. *The Higher Aspects of Greek Religion*. London, 1912 (reprinted 1977).

Feaver, Douglas D. "Historical Development in the Priesthoods of Athens." *YCS* 15 (1957), 123–158.

Ferguson, William S. "The Salaminioi of Heptaphylai and Sounion." *Hesperia* 7 (1938), 1–74.

Fontenrose, Joseph. *The Delphic Oracle*. Berkeley, 1978.

François, Gilbert. *Le Polythéisme et l'emploi au singulier des mots Θεός, Δαίμων*. Paris, 1957.

Fustel de Coulanges, Numa D. *The Ancient City*. Paris, 1864 (English translation, 1873).

Gernet, Louis, and Boulanger, André. *Le Génie grec dans la religion*. Paris, 1932 (reprinted 1969).

Glotz, Gustave. *La Solidarité de la famille*. Paris, 1904 (reprinted 1973).

Gordon, Richard. "Fear of Freedom? Selective Continuity in Religion during the Hellenistic Period." *Didaskalos* 4 (1972), 48–60.

Guarducci, Margherita. "L'Istituzione della fratria." *Memorie della classe di scienze morali e storiche dell' Accademia dei Lincei*, ser. 6, 6, fasc. 1 (1937), 27–41.

Guthrie, William K. C. *The Greeks and Their Gods*. London, 1950.

————. *A History of Greek Philosophy*. 6 vols. Cambridge, 1962–1981.

Habicht, Christian. *Gottmenschentum und griechische Städte*. Munich, 1970.

Halliday, William R. *Greek Divination*. London, 1913.

Hamdorf, Friedrich W. *Griechische Kultpersonifikationen der vorhellenistischen Zeit*. Mainz, 1964.

Harrison, Alick R. W. *The Law of Athens*. 2 vols. Oxford, 1968–1971.

Haussoullier, Bernard C. L. M. *La Vie municipale en Attique*. Paris, 1884 (reprinted 1979).

Hewitt, Joseph W. "On the Development of the Thank-Offering among the Greeks." *TAPA* 43 (1942), 95–111.

Jacoby, Felix. *Die Fragmente der griechischen Historiker*. 3 vols. in 14 parts. Berlin and Leiden, 1923–1958.

Jeanmaire, Henri. *Couroi et Courètes*. Lille, 1939 (reprinted 1975).

Jones, William H. S. "A Note on the Vague Use of ΘΕΟΣ." *CR* 27 (1913), 252–255.

Jörgensen, Ove. "Das Auftreten der Götter in den Büchern ι–μ der Odyssee." *Hermes* 39 (1904), 357–382.

Kennedy, George E. *The Art of Persuasion in Greece.* Princeton, 1963.

Kern, Otto. *Die Religion der Griechen.* 3 vols. Berlin, 1926–1938.

Kron, Uta. *Die zehn attischen Phylenheroen.* Berlin, 1976.

Kurtz, Donna C., and Boardman, John. *Greek Burial Customs.* London, 1971.

Lacey, William K. *The Family in Classical Greece.* London, 1968.

Latte, Kurt. *Heiliges Recht.* Tübingen, 1920 (reprinted 1964).

———. "Phratrie." *RE* 20 (1941), cols. 746–758.

———. "Schuld und Sünde in der griechischen Religion." *Archiv für Religionswissenschaft* 20 (1920–1921), 254–298.

Lattimore, Richmond A. *Themes in Greek and Latin Epitaphs.* Urbana, 1962.

Linforth, Ivan M. "Named and Unnamed Gods in Herodotus." *University of California Publications in Classical Philology* 9 (1928), 201–243.

Lloyd-Jones, Hugh. *The Justice of Zeus.* Berkeley, 1971.

Lonis, Raoul. *Guerre et religion en Grèce à l'époque classique.* Paris, 1979.

MacDowell, Douglas M. *Andokides: On the Mysteries.* Oxford, 1962.

———. *Athenian Homicide Law.* Manchester, 1963.

MacKendrick, Paul L. *The Athenian Aristocracy.* Cambridge, Massachusetts, 1969.

Meier, Carl A. "The Dream in Ancient Greece." In *The Dream and Human Societies,* edited by Gustave E. von Grunebaum and Roger Caillois, 303–319. Berkeley, 1966.

Meuss, Heinrich. "Die Vorstellungen von Gottheit und Schicksal bei den attischen Rednern." *Jahrbücher für classische Philologie* 139 (1889), 445–476.

Mikalson, Jon D. "Religion in the Attic Demes." *AJP* 98 (1977), 424–435.

———. *The Sacred and Civil Calendar of the Athenian Year.* Princeton, 1975.

Mossé, Claude. *Athens in Decline 404–86 B.C.* Paris, 1962 (English translation, 1973).

Moulinier, Louis. *Le Pur et l'impur dans la pensée des Grecs.* Paris, 1952 (reprinted 1975).

Mylonas, George E. *Eleusis and the Eleusinian Mysteries.* Princeton, 1962.

Nagelsbach, Karl F. *Die nachhomerische Theologie.* Nuremberg, 1857.

Nestle, Wilhelm. *Griechische Religiosität.* 3 vols. Berlin, 1930–1934.

Nilsson, Martin P. *Cults, Myths, Oracles, and Politics in Ancient Greece.* Lund, 1951 (reprinted 1972).

———. *Geschichte der griechischen Religion,* vol. 1³. Munich, 1967.

———. *Greek Folk Religion.* New York, 1940 (reprinted 1971).

———. *Greek Piety.* Oxford, 1948.

———. *A History of Greek Religion².* Oxford, 1952 (reprinted 1964).

Nock, Arthur D. *Arthur Darby Nock: Essays on Religion and the Ancient World.* Edited by Zeph Stewart. 2 vols. Cambridge, Mass., 1972.

———. *Conversion.* Oxford, 1933 (reprinted 1952).

———. "The Cult of Heroes." *HTR* 37 (1944), 141–174.

———. "Religious Attitudes of the Ancient Greeks." *Proceedings of the American Philosophical Society* 85 (1942), 472–482.

Oliver, James H. *The Athenian Expounders of the Sacred and Ancestral Law.* Baltimore, 1950.

Parke, Herbert W. *Festivals of the Athenians.* London, 1977.

———. *The Oracles of Zeus.* Oxford, 1967.

———, and Wormell, Donald E. W. *The Delphic Oracle.* 2 vols. Oxford, 1956.

Peek, Werner. *Griechische Vers-Inschriften,* vol. 1. Berlin, 1955.

———. *Kerameikos,* vol. 3. Berlin, 1941.

Pfister, Friedrich. "Epiphanie." *RE* suppl. 4 (1924), cols. 277–323.

———. "Kultus." *RE* 11 (1922), cols. 2120–2123.

Plescia, Joseph. *The Oath and Perjury in Ancient Greece.* Tallahassee, 1970.

Popp, Harald F. *Die Einwirkung von Vorzeichen, Opfern, und Festen auf die Kriegführung der Griechen im 5. und 4. Jahrhundert v. Chr.* Würzburg, 1957.

Pritchett, William K. *The Greek State at War.* 3 vols. Berkeley, 1974–1980.

Reverdin, Olivier. *La Religion de la cité platonicienne.* Paris, 1945.

Rohde, Erwin. *Psyche*[8]. Translated by W. B. Hillis. London, 1925 (reprinted 1966).

Rose, Herbert J. "The Religion of a Greek Household." *Euphrosyne* 1 (1957), 95–116.

Rouse, William H. D. *Greek Votive Offerings.* Cambridge, 1912.

Roussel, Denis. *Tribu et cité.* Paris, 1976.

Rudhardt, Jean. *Notions fondamentales de la pensée religieuse et actes constitutifs du culte dans la Grèce classique.* Geneva, 1958.

———. "Religion sociale et religion personnelle dans la Grèce antique." *Dialectica* 30 (1976), 267–276.

Schlaifer, Robert. "Notes on Athenian Public Cults." *HSCP* 51 (1940), 233–260.

Sjövall, Harald. *Zeus im altgriechischen Hauskult.* Lund, 1931.

Solders, Severin. *Die ausserstädtischen Kulte und die Einigung Attikas.* Lund, 1931.

Tod, Marcus N. *A Selection of Greek Historical Inscriptions.* 2 vols. Oxford, 1946–1948.

Toepffer, Johannes A. F. *Attische Genealogie.* Berlin, 1889 (reprinted 1973).

Wachsmuth, Dietrich. "Epiphanie." *Kleine Pauly* 5 (1975), cols. 1598–1601.

Walzer, Richard. "Sulla religione di Senofonte." *Annali della Scuola Normale Superiore di Pisa,* ser. 2, 5 (1936), 17–32.

Wevers, Richard F. *Isaeus.* The Hague, 1969.

Wilamowitz, Ulrich von. *Der Glaube der Hellenen.* 2 vols. Berlin, 1931–1932 (reprinted 1959).

Wünsch, Richard. *Defixionum Tabellae in Attica Regione Repertae,* in *IG* III.3. Berlin, 1897.

Wycherley, Richard E. *The Stones of Athens.* Princeton, 1978.

Wyse, William. *The Speeches of Isaeus.* Cambridge, 1904 (reprinted 1967).

INDEX OF
PASSAGES CITED

Texts

Curse Tablets

GENERAL INDEX